THE
SELF-
REGULATION
WORKBOOK FOR KIDS

THE SELF-REGULATION WORKBOOK FOR KIDS

CBT Exercises and **Coping Strategies** to Help Children Handle Anxiety, Stress, and Other Strong Emotions

Jenna Berman, LCSW

ULYSSES BOOKS
FOR YOUNG READERS

Published by:
Ulysses Books for Young Readers,
an imprint of Ulysses Press
PO Box 3440
Berkeley, CA 94703
www.ulyssespress.com

ISBN: 978-1-64604-183-1
Library of Congress Control Number: 2021931486

Printed in the United States
10 9 8 7 6 5

Acquisitions editor: Casie Vogel
Managing editor: Claire Chun
Project editor: Renee Rutledge
Proofreader: Barbara Schultz
Front cover design: Justin Shirley
Cover artwork: © shutterstock.com © lineartestpilota; © artnLera; © Freud;
  © kostolom3000; © indratw; © Mbukimbuki
Interior design: what!design @ whatweb.com
Layout and production: Jake Flaherty
Interior art: shutterstock.com © Keigo Yasuda; © Nata Lima; © drawkman;
  © Jimena Catalina Gayo; © Micro One; © Ozant; © Colorfuel Studio; © greenpic studio

CONTENTS

INTRODUCTION

Teaching children how to identify, understand, and be in control of their thinking, mood, and behavior is crucial to their ability to self-regulate. This book introduces these skills in a child-friendly manner through both story and activities. While this workbook is intended for children ages eight through eleven, the tools and skills, especially those related to identifying and challenging unhelpful thoughts, are valuable for people of all ages and may be advanced for children younger than eight.

When children struggle with self-regulation, it often leads to behaviors that make them feel even worse and create stressful situations for others. While children typically regret such behavior and don't want to repeat it, they likely don't have the skills to be able to react differently when faced with a similar trigger in the future. This workbook helps children to develop the skills to be able to:

- Identify, understand, and express their feelings

- Learn to calm their body

- Identify and challenge unhelpful thoughts

- Identify unhelpful behavior and more adaptive choices they can make instead

- Identify and prepare for situations that may be tricky for them to navigate

These skills are the foundation of cognitive behavioral therapy (CBT), an evidence-based treatment that helps people to improve their functioning when dealing with a wide range of problems. Through CBT—which has a decades-old canon of nonproprietary clinical terms and techniques that are elaborated upon throughout this book—people can learn how to recognize their triggers, become aware of their Automatic Thoughts and responses to them, and learn more adaptive ways of thinking and reacting.

In this workbook, a character named Alex will tell the story of his journey learning and using different tools and techniques to take control of his feelings. There are a number of activities to help your child learn, practice, and internalize the concepts. Read Alex's story aloud with your child and support them in completing the activities. There are side notes for grown-ups throughout the book, which is applicable to teachers, mentors, and clinicians as well as parents and caregivers to support their work with kids. These are not intended to be read with your child. While none of the information provided in these side notes would be harmful for a child to learn, they are directed toward adults and are likely to be confusing and boring for them. Alex is a fictional and hypothetical character. Any resemblance he may bear toward an actual child or children is purely coincidental. All of the lessons provided in the book work for Alex, whereas each and every tool or technique may not be efficacious for your child.

Keep in mind that developing a skill takes time and practice. Be patient and provide your child with the necessary support to be able to use these skills in their everyday environment. This can include verbal reminders, visual reminders, and actually going through the steps of a skill or plan with them.

Spelling, grammar, and penmanship don't count when it comes to exercises to help manage emotions. If these are challenging or triggering for your child, consider allowing them to complete the exercises verbally and then writing their responses. If that is difficult for your child, you can read the text together and make up other ways to process and further explore the content, such as acting it out or telling a story about it with toys. Meet your child where they're at and adapt the lessons for them. Simply thinking and talking about tricky or unmanageable thoughts, feelings, and behaviors is challenging enough!

It is important for you and your child to further discuss the content of the book and find opportunities to connect it to real-life situations, both while reading and as you're living your lives. Additionally, practice the skills repeatedly to help your child internalize them. This will support your child's ability to access the tools when they are actually faced with intense emotions that are difficult to manage.

Even when a child has made progress, he or she will continue at times to make mistakes and act on their overwhelming emotions—or allow their "feelings to get in control." These instances can be opportunities to continue learning and growing. Taking control of feelings is a lifelong process. Even I, a grown-up who helps people manage their emotions for a living, have moments when my feelings get in control and I react in ways that I regret later! This is part of being human. Anticipating this can help make these moments more tolerable. It's stressful for your child when this happens as well. Be sure to instill messages that decrease feelings of shame. When children have difficulty with self-regulation, they often get messages that their behavior is bad, and they develop an underlying belief that they are bad. Help your child understand that even when their behavior is not good at times, they are always a good person who has strengths. Regulating emotions is hard. It's harder for some people than it is for others, and that's okay. You will work together to help your child build the skills to be able to regulate emotions better.

Chapter 1 will help your child to expand their emotions vocabulary, understand that it is normal to experience a wide range of emotions, think about what triggers these emotions and how they affect their functioning, and view emotions as something that they can do something about. Having a larger emotions vocabulary can help a child more accurately identify and understand both their experiences and the experiences of others. This improves a child's ability to manage their emotions and develop healthier relationships. Learning that it is normal to experience a wide range of feelings can help children to feel more comfortable acknowledging and addressing their own emotions and to be more empathetic and tolerant when interacting with others.

Chapter 2 will teach your child to think about the intensity of their emotions. Increased awareness of the ability to experience both pleasant and unpleasant feelings at different levels of intensity can help your child to work toward having less frequent big reactions to small triggers and to calm down more quickly.

Chapter 3 will help your child to differentiate between experiences, thoughts, feelings, and behaviors. We live in a society that tends to jumble up these things. It is important to realize that our thoughts and feelings are not facts. This will set the foundation for your child to be able to do the work later.

Chapter 4 will teach your child to recognize the way that emotions effect their body.

Chapter 5 will teach a number of tools that can help your child to relax and take control of those feelings in their body. Calming down automatic physical responses to emotions will help your child to improve their ability to control their reactions.

Chapter 6 will teach your child to be able to notice their Automatic Thoughts and recognize when they are unhelpful.

Chapter 7 will teach your child how to challenge and reshape their unhelpful thoughts. The ability to identify and challenge unhelpful thinking can allow your child to view stressful situations more clearly and navigate them more effectively.

Chapter 8 will help your child increase their awareness of the fact that their actions are choices that they can thoughtfully make. After your child develops an understanding of their ability to have an urge and be in control at the same time.

Chapter 9 will introduce them to tools that can support their ability to choose their actions.

Chapters 10 and **11** will help your child to connect all of the tools and insights that they developed as they completed the earlier sections of the workbook. In Chapter 10, your child will write a story about a time when their feelings were in control. Through this activity, your child will further process and internalize the connection between a trigger, their Automatic Thoughts about it, emotions, and reactions. In Chapter 11, your child will rewrite that same story by inserting the coping skills learned to manage the same unhelpful automatic thoughts and urges. If your child writes this story about a trigger that is actually challenging for them to deal with, this can help them prepare to deal with a similar trigger when they are faced with it in the future. Writing stories about coping with common triggers in a healthy manner and reviewing these stories can help your child to internalize the insights, tools, and skills that can be helpful in such situations. This will support their ability to recall this information and apply it to real-life situations.

Chapter 12 provides your child with a helpful self-statement and image to instill a sense of empowerment in their ability to navigate the stressors that come their way.

If your child continues to struggle with self-regulation, seek the support of a trained mental health clinician. Therapy can help you and your child to process and understand their unique, complex thoughts, feelings, and behaviors. Additionally, having your child complete a neuropsychological evaluation can help to better understand the lagging skills contributing to their difficulties so that you can get them set up with the appropriate supports.

CHAPTER 1
IDENTIFYING AND UNDERSTANDING FEELINGS

Hi! I'm Alex, and I'm a kid just like you! I live in a house with my mom, my dad, my sister Sammy, and my cat Toby. I love reading, riding my bike, and going to the park. Every day, I experience lots of different feelings. I have probably experienced thousands of different shades of all kinds of feelings! My mom, dad, and sister experience feelings too. In fact, every person around the world experiences all different feelings, both pleasant and unpleasant. And that's okay! In this book, I'm going to tell you about my journey experiencing big feelings and how I learned to take control of them. There will be activities to help you learn and practice the tools and skills that helped me to take control of my feelings. I hope these tools and skills are helpful for you too!

When we're dealing with our emotions and feelings, it's important to be able to name them. That way we can talk about them with our friends and family and decide how we want to deal with them. These are a few of the feelings that I have experienced:

Bored Proud Eager
Amazed Silly
Confused
Relieved
Scared Content
Bitter Inspired

ACTIVITY
COLOR THE FEELINGS FACES

Color the feelings faces. These are just some of the many feelings that people experience. Learning and thinking about different feelings can help us to figure out our own feelings. When we really understand what we are feeling, it makes it easier to decide what to do about it.

Happy

Angry

Proud

Frustrated

Worried

Sad

THE SELF-REGULATION WORKBOOK FOR KIDS

Disgusted

Relieved

Surprised

Bored

Embarrassed

Confused

Excited

◇◇◇◇

NOTE TO THE GROWN-UPS: Find opportunities to label feelings for your child. Tell them when you are experiencing an emotion and why you are feeling it. For example, "I am feeling happy because I like reading with you" or "I am feeling frustrated because I forgot to get eggs at the grocery store." Label feelings your child might be experiencing. For example, "You are feeling disappointed that there are no swings available for you to play on" or "It seems like you are feeling excited to do this craft." Labeling feelings can help children to better understand them. When you label your child's feelings, it can help them to accept them and to feel validated. Additionally, once a feeling is identified, it can give the child a chance to make sense of what they are experiencing and transform the emotion from something happening to them to something over which they can take control.

Sometimes I get the message that I shouldn't have certain feelings.

But I know that it's okay to experience all feelings. It's not fun to experience some feelings, but it's normal and healthy. Everyone has unpleasant feelings sometimes! I'm not alone when I feel that way. Even unpleasant feelings can be good for me when I am in control of them. If I didn't have these feelings sometimes, then I would be a robot!

NOTE TO THE GROWN-UPS: While it is natural to want to protect children from experiencing unpleasant emotions, it is important to remember that these emotions are healthy. Experiencing unpleasant emotions helps your child to build their tolerance for the inevitable stressful experiences of life and to develop healthy coping and problem-solving skills.

When I ignore my feelings, they don't go away. I just bottle up the feelings. When I bottle up my feelings, it is harder to deal with them.

ACTIVITY
FILLING UP MY FEELINGS CUP

It's time to do an activity with a grown-up! You are going to use a cup and water to explore how feelings sometimes "overflow." This activity involves spilling water on the ground, so be sure to do it in a place and at a time that a grown-up approves.

Have you ever felt like you can't hold your feelings in any longer, and they're just pouring out? This activity will help you to understand why that sometimes happens and why it's important to deal with our feelings instead of trying to ignore them. As you do this activity, imagine that the cup is your Feelings Cup, and the water is feelings. Gather the following materials and have a grown-up walk you through the steps and read you the story to think about what happens when we try to bottle up our feelings.

Materials

- A cup
- A pitcher of water

Instructions

1. Go outside or somewhere that your grown-up doesn't mind water spilling.

2. Have your grown-up put a little water into the cup. This will be bottled-up feelings.

3. Hold the cup. Walk back and forth as quickly as possible. Try not to let the water spill out of the cup. While you're doing this, have your grown-up request the following (but don't peek at them before you do this!):

   o Name a color
   o Name a shape
   o Name a fruit
   o Name a vegetable

4. Read this story:

- One morning, I was sleeping when I was suddenly awoken by my mom shouting, "Wake up! We're late!" I felt surprised and scared.

5. Have your grown-up pour more water into the cup to show the new feelings.

6. Hold the cup. Walk back and forth as quickly as possible, trying your hardest not to spill the water. (Note: Some water will eventually spill out—that's normal and okay.) While you're doing this, have your grown-up request the following:

- Name a sport
- Name a song
- Name a book
- Name a movie

7. Read more of the story:

I got dressed as quickly as possible, and we rushed to school. When I got to school, I realized that I forgot my homework. I felt upset.

8. Have your grown-up pour more water into the cup to show the new feelings.

9. Hold the cup. Walk back and forth as quickly as possible. Have your grown-up ask you the following questions:

- Name a farm animal
- Name an underwater animal
- Name a jungle animal
- Name a pet

10. Continue reading the story:

- When we were lining up to go to art class, I tripped and fell. Another kid laughed and said, "You're so clumsy!" I felt embarrassed.

11. Have your grown-up pour more water into the cup to show the new feelings.

12. Hold the cup. Walk back and forth as quickly as possible. Have your grown-up request the following:

- o Name a family member
- o Name a teacher
- o Name a month
- o Name a holiday

13. Keep reading the story:

- o At lunch, my friend asked, "Are you okay?" I told her about my day so far. She said, "Wow! What a day! I'm glad all of that is over! I hope all of those feelings pass soon." That made me feel a lot better.

14. Pour half of the water in the cup back into the pitcher.

15. Hold the cup. Walk back and forth as quickly as possible. Have your grown-up request the following:

- o Name a season
- o Name a day of the week
- o Name a bug
- o Name a flower

16. Read more of the story:

- o During recess, I played four square. It was so much fun! I totally forgot about my stressful morning and moved on with my day!

17. Pour the rest of the water in the cup back into the pitcher.

18. Hold the empty cup. Walk back and forth as quickly as possible. Have your grown-up request the following:

- o Name an ice cream flavor
- o Name a candy
- o Name a drink
- o Name an item of clothing

19. Good job! You've completed the most challenging part of this activity! Now think about this:

○ How much water did you end up spilling?

  If you spilled a lot of water, that's okay and totally normal! Pretend the water spilling out was a Feelings Explosion. A Feelings Explosion is when you act on your emotions and do something without thinking first, such as whining, pouting, throwing a tantrum, yelling at someone, or running away from something.

○ Did it get more challenging to walk fast when the cup was filled higher? Did it get more challenging to answer the questions when the cup was filled higher?

  If you answered yes, that makes sense! It takes a lot of focus and energy to try to keep a cup filled with water from spilling. When we bottle up our feelings, it also gets more challenging to do things and think. That's because it takes a lot of energy to hold in our feelings, even when we don't realize it!

◇◇◇◇

When I bottle up my emotions, I have bigger reactions to smaller things that happen. For example, one day I was feeling embarrassed, sad, ashamed, and anxious about something that happened in school. I bottled up those feelings. Later, when I was home, my sister Sammy started singing. I asked her to stop, and she responded, "Relax, Alex," and kept singing. I felt very annoyed very fast and yelled at her. It was as if I had no more room left in my Feelings Cup for the annoyance that her singing triggered, so all of the feelings that I was holding inside came pouring out. I call this a Feelings Explosion.

Yelling at my sister just created more problems. We got into a fight and then I got in trouble. That made me feel upset on top of everything else! The next day, I moved on from all of the feelings that I had been bottling up. When my sister started singing, it still annoyed me but the feelings weren't as strong, and it was easier to just ignore.

Thinking about the emotions that we are holding onto can help us to deal with them instead of just letting them overflow. When we ignore our feelings, they usually don't simply go away. Being aware of our feelings helps us to stay in control of them.

ACTIVITY
HOW FULL IS MY FEELINGS CUP?

Think about how full your Feelings Cup is right now. Draw a line across the cup to illustrate this. For example, if you're holding onto a lot of feelings, draw a line at the top of the cup. If you are not feeling very emotional right now, draw a line toward the bottom of the cup. Write the emotions that you are feeling inside and/or around the cup.

◇◇◇◇

When our Feelings Cup is full, we can do things to empty it out a little bit. Here are some of the things I like to do when I notice that my Feelings Cup is getting full:

- Talk to someone about my feelings
- Give someone a hug
- Write in a journal
- Paint a picture
- Play with or pet my cat
- Take a bath
- Put an ice pack on my neck
- Dance
- Do 100 jumping jacks
- Sing
- Listen to music
- Read
- Play an instrument

I'll teach you even more of my favorite coping tools that help me to empty out my Feelings Cup later, but it's important to notice and use the tools that we already have to help us manage our feelings!

ACTIVITY
MY TOOL KIT FOR MANAGING FEELINGS

Write a list of the things that you do to help you feel calm and relaxed. You can use ideas from my list and add your own. As you continue to do this workbook and learn more ways to manage feelings, you can add to the list. When you start to notice that your Feelings Cup is full, refer back to this list to help you choose how to deal with the feelings.

Sometimes it seems like my feelings take control of me. My feelings can make me have thoughts that aren't true and aren't helpful. It's almost like my feelings turn into a little Feelings Monster in my head telling me these unhelpful thoughts. For example, if I make a mistake, the Feelings Monster might say, "You can't do anything right!"

Feelings can also make me want to do things that aren't good for me and may even cause bigger problems that make me feel worse. It's like the Feelings Monster takes over my body like I'm a puppet. For example, I might start crying and yelling. Has this ever happened to you?

Let me tell you a story about a time this happened to me...

One day, I was building a super-big, magical castle out of blocks. I had been working on it for hours and felt really proud and excited about how it was coming along.

My sister ran into the room, threw a ball toward me, and shouted, "Think fast, Alex!" I missed the ball and it flew right into my castle, knocking it down. I thought, "My castle is ruined! I have been working on this all day! My whole day is ruined!" and felt sad. A tear rolled down my cheek.

My sister said, "Don't cry. It's just blocks." I thought, "Just blocks?! It was a super-big, magical castle that I worked really hard on! She's so mean!" I felt angry. I picked up a block and threw it at my sister.

While I thought my whole day was ruined, it really wasn't. While I thought my sister was a mean person, this moment did not really change the person she is. She might say and do things that I think are mean sometimes, but she's not a mean person. These thoughts made me feel even sadder and angrier.

I had the urge to throw the block at my sister because I felt so angry. Making this choice caused me to get in trouble, and then I felt even more upset. I let my feelings take control, and that just caused bigger problems.

When we learn how to understand our feelings, thinking, and behavior, we gain the power to take control of them!

Learning about and understanding my triggers helped me to take control of my feelings, thinking, and behavior. A trigger is a situation, person, place, or thing that leads to a reaction. Our reactions can include emotions, thoughts, feelings in our bodies, and behaviors. For example, cleaning my room is a trigger for me to feel bored. Walking by my favorite ice cream shop is a trigger that makes me think, "I want to eat ice cream." Someone tickling me is a trigger that makes me laugh. It is helpful to think about the triggers that lead to different feelings, especially when it comes to feelings that are hard to manage! When we are aware of our triggers, it helps us to stop and think before reacting to them!

ACTIVITY
FEELINGS CUBE

You are going to make and play a game with a Feelings Cube. Identifying our triggers can give us the power to come up with and try to follow a plan to take control of our feelings when we are faced with the triggers.

Instructions

1. Color the faces on the Feelings Cube on page 21.

2. Fold the dotted lines.

3. Use tape to put the cube together.

4. Take turns rolling the Feelings Cube. When you land on a feeling, say something that would trigger you to experience that feeling. For example, if I landed on WORRIED, I could say, "Something that triggers me to feel worried is taking spelling tests."

5. Fill in the triggers on the Feelings Cube chart on page 20.

FEELINGS CHART

Fill in the triggers for each feeling that you roll.

HAPPY	PROUD	WORRIED	ANGRY	SAD	EMBARRASSED
		Example: Taking spelling tests			

NOW TRY THIS: After you've written down triggers based on what you've rolled, add any other triggers that might cause the different feelings.

NOTE TO THE GROWN-UPS: It can sometimes be difficult to understand a child's feelings. It is important to acknowledge and empathize with emotions and resist the urge to challenge them, even when the emotions seem inappropriate to the situation. As humans, our thoughts and feelings aren't good or bad—they just *are*. This is an important belief to instill in children. When children get the message that their emotions are wrong, it can trigger them to feel other emotions such as confusion, guilt, frustration, and shame on top of what they were already experiencing. This can make it even more challenging for the child to manage their emotions.

THE SELF-REGULATION WORKBOOK FOR KIDS

ACTIVITY
WHAT AM I FEELING? CARDS

Draw a picture to represent each of the feelings on the following feelings cards. Cut them out of the book and place them in an envelope. When you experience a feeling, you can look at the cards to help you figure out what you are feeling. Identifying your feelings in the moment can help you to take control of them!

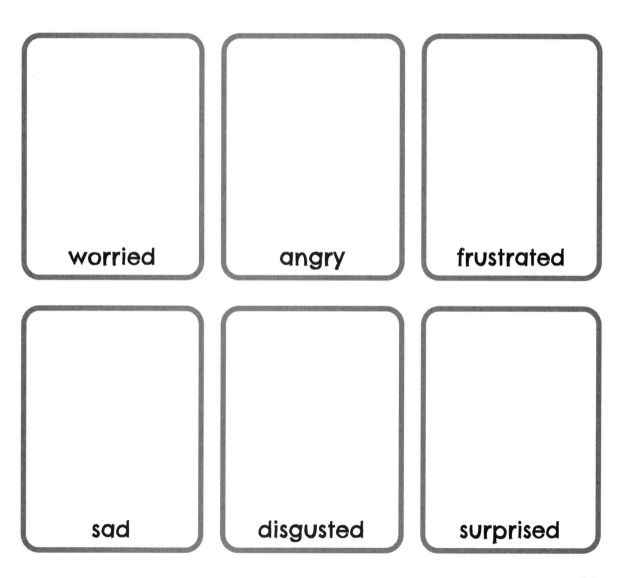

worried

angry

frustrated

sad

disgusted

surprised

THE SELF-REGULATION WORKBOOK FOR KIDS

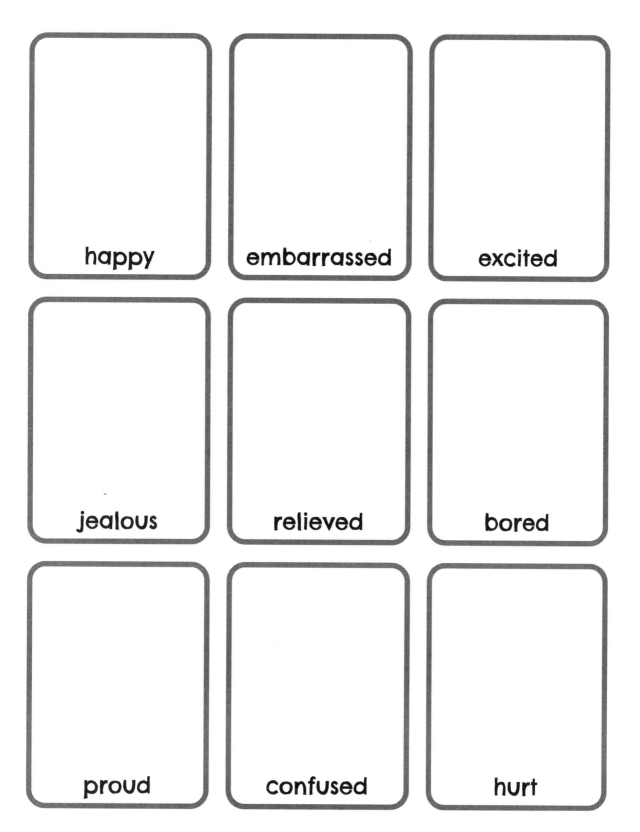

happy

embarrassed

excited

jealous

relieved

bored

proud

confused

hurt

CHAPTER 2
THE STRENGTH OF FEELINGS

Sometimes my feelings are big, and sometimes my feelings are small. I like to think about rating how strong my feelings are with a Feelings Thermometer!

I'll show you what I mean…

This Is a Feelings Thermometer:

I can rate the strength of any feeling on the Feelings Thermometer!

Check out some things I've felt on the *Joy Thermometer*:

I feel a **9** of joy celebrating at my birthday party.

I feel a **7** of joy when I go to the beach with my family.

I feel a **5** of joy when I play with my friends during recess.

I feel a **3** of joy when I pass a cute dog on the street.

I feel a **1** of joy when I eat a yummy breakfast in the morning.

And here are some things I've felt on the *Frustration* Thermometer:

10	I feel a **9** of frustration when the trip I had been looking forward to gets canceled.
9	
8	I feel a **7** of frustration when I try really hard to do a trick and have trouble doing it.
7	
6	I feel a **5** of frustration when I do not understand the lesson in school.
5	
4	I feel a **3** of frustration when I have to wait for a long time for my turn in kickball.
3	
2	I feel a **1** of frustration when I stub my toe.
1	

ACTIVITY
FILL IN THE FEELINGS THERMOMETERS

On the following pages, you will find a happiness thermometer, proud thermometer, sadness thermometer, worry thermometer, and anger thermometer. Fill in the thermometers with events that trigger different levels of each of the feelings.

Happiness

10
9
8
7
6
5
4
3
2
1

NOTE TO THE GROWN-UPS: Sometimes it might be hard to understand how a certain situation can trigger such intense emotions for your child. You might think that the intensity of their emotional reaction is inappropriate and they are "over-feeling." It is important to remember that whether or not the intensity of the emotions make sense to you, they are still very real and difficult for your child to experience. These intense emotions might make more sense once you begin to understand the Automatic Thoughts that your child has during these moments. Stay tuned for more about this later in Chapter 6!

Proud

```
10
 9
 8
 7
 6
 5
 4
 3
 2
 1
```

_____
_____
_____
_____
_____
_____
_____
_____
_____

Sadness

```
10
 9
 8
 7
 6
 5
 4
 3
 2
 1
```

_____
_____
_____
_____
_____
_____
_____
_____
_____

Worry

```
10
9
8
7
6
5
4
3
2
1
```

_____
_____
_____
_____
_____
_____
_____
_____
_____

Anger

```
10
9
8
7
6
5
4
3
2
1
```

_____
_____
_____
_____
_____
_____
_____
_____
_____

THE SELF-REGULATION WORKBOOK FOR KIDS

Try filling out a Feelings Thermometer of your own!

Feeling: _____

```
10
 9
 8
 7
 6
 5
 4
 3
 2
 1
```

_____
_____
_____
_____
_____
_____
_____
_____
_____
_____

NOTE TO THE GROWN-UPS: A handy way to help your child regularly think about and use the Feelings Thermometer is to print one out and either laminate it or put it in a sheet protector. Your child can then use a dry erase marker to write the feeling that they are rating and mark how intensely they are experiencing it on the thermometer. After your child does something to try to manage the feeling, such as talking to someone or doing something to relax, they can then reevaluate how intensely they are experiencing the feeling on the thermometer. It is helpful for your them to see when their feelings are chilling out, whether it's because of something they actively did to take control of the feeling or because of time passing.

I like rating positive feelings such as when I'm happy and proud on the Feelings Thermometer. Sometimes this helps me realize that even days that feel crummy aren't all bad. I'll tell you a story to show you what I mean…

The day was finally here–we were going to have a big scavenger hunt in the park with our friends! I looked out the window and saw that it was dark and rainy outside. My mom told me that the scavenger hunt was canceled. I felt disappointed. I went into the kitchen for breakfast, poured a bowl of my favorite cereal, and then spilled it all over the floor. That was the last of the cereal, so I had to eat something else. I felt frustrated. Sammy and I decided to watch a movie. Just as we started, the power went out. I felt annoyed. Later that day, I tripped. My foot really hurt! I had to get an x-ray. I felt nervous. Then the doctor told me that I needed to wear a cast for the next 6 weeks. I felt so upset! Before bed, I said, "Today was a crummy day!" My dad agreed that there were things that day that were crummy. Then we talked about some of the things that happened during the day that were not crummy... After the power went out, Sammy and I made a huge fort and spent hours reading books and playing inside. That made me feel a 5 of happiness and a 6 of pride! I got to pick out a cool color for my cast. That made me feel a 1 of happiness. Sammy and my parents signed it. I was looking forward to having my friends sign it too. That made me feel a 2 of happiness. I had my favorite pizza for dinner and an ice cream sundae for dessert. That made me feel a 3 of happiness. While there were things that were crummy that day, there were also a lot of things that brought me joy! Noticing these things helped to make me feel a little bit less bad about my day.

NOTE TO THE GROWN-UPS: Encouraging your child to acknowledge the little joys can support them in experiencing more joy and positive emotions. Experiencing more positive emotions can help to make negative emotions more tolerable.

ACTIVITY
JOY JOURNAL

Every night before you go to bed this week, write down at least one thing that brought you joy during the day in the Joy Journal below.

DAY	THE THING(S) THAT BROUGHT ME JOY	FEELINGS THERMOMETER RATING

◇◇◇◇

Dealing with Strong Feelings

It is helpful to rate the negative feelings I experience too. When I notice how strong my negative feelings are, it helps me to decide how to deal with them. I used to think that I couldn't handle feeling angry or sad at all. When I felt just a little bit angry, it felt terrible! When I started thinking about how strong my anger was on the Feelings Thermometer, I realized that some anger is uncomfortable and I don't like it, but it's not that big a deal. For example, I feel angry when it's my sister's turn to choose the game we are going to play. When I thought about it and rated my feelings on the thermometer, I realized that this was only a 2 of anger. I can tolerate a 2 of anger! Tolerate is a big word that means I can deal with it. Humans can tolerate things, even when they're uncomfortable!

When I rate my feelings on the Feelings Thermometer, it helps me to decide what to do. I choose to deal with problems differently depending on how strong the feelings are. We'll talk more about that later. Sometimes it's handy to use the Feelings Thermometer to notice that even if a feeling or problem didn't go away, I feel less bad about it. I like to use the Feelings Thermometer after every effort I make to cope with my feelings. Noticing if my feelings chilled out even a little bit can help me to realize that the feelings are going to pass. It also helps me to remember that while I can't control the things that happen, I can control the ways that I think and the things that I do, which gives me the power to take control of my feelings! We are going to keep using the Feelings Thermometer as we learn more tools and tricks to take control of feelings.

NOTE TO THE GROWN-UPS: Everyone has a threshold of what they are able to tolerate. Sometimes it is challenging for children to tolerate even mild emotions. Sometimes it is difficult for adults to watch the children they care about experience even mild emotions. As children gain experience navigating stressful situations and learn how to identify and understand their feelings, they can strengthen their ability to tolerate and cope with a range of emotions. When gently pushing your child to confront stressful situations, you can explain that facing them will help to build the skills to take control of whatever feelings and situations come their way. You can assure your child that you will be there as a safety net to catch them if they fall while trying their hardest to deal with the stressful situations.

ACTIVITY
HOLDING ICE

Experiencing unpleasant emotions like sadness, frustration, anger, and embarrassment can be uncomfortable. Holding a piece of ice in your hand can be uncomfortable too. Let's see how much discomfort from holding the ice you can tolerate!

Get a piece of ice and hold it in one hand. Have your grown-up set an alarm for 5 minutes. The ice is going to feel cold! See if you can tolerate the discomfort of holding the ice in your one hand for the entire 5 minutes. If it starts to feel too uncomfortable for you, try coming up with things that you can do to feel a little bit more comfortable while holding it until the 5 minutes are up. When you're done, talk about these questions with your grown-up:

- Were you able to hold the ice at all when it felt uncomfortable?

- How did you decide if it was too uncomfortable for you to keep holding the ice?

- What were some of the things you did to make it feel a little bit more comfortable to hold the ice?

- Let's pretend it got even more uncomfortable to hold the ice but you couldn't put it down. Think of as many ideas as possible to try to deal with this. Get creative! Hint: Problem-solving can include using different materials and asking for help.

Just like you were able to tolerate the discomfort of holding an ice cube, you can also tolerate the discomfort of experiencing unpleasant feelings! You can problem-solve and ask for help when feelings are hard to deal with on your own.

◇◇◇◇

NOTE TO THE GROWN-UPS: Some children experience emotions more intensely than others. While it can be overwhelming to experience such intense emotions and difficult to learn how to manage them, emotional intensity can be a wonderful strength. Children who are highly sensitive may experience all emotions more intensely. Being highly passionate, caring, empathetic, and attentive can help drive a child to do great things. Even emotions such as anger can motivate them to try to make a difference in powerful ways.

Children need to learn how to understand and manage their emotions, which takes time and support, especially when feelings are strong. Because behaviors that are shaped by intense emotions can be distressing for all, highly sensitive children often get the message that they are too emotional, too dramatic, too timid, or too much. When a child receives these messages, they may internalize a sense of shame that can significantly impact their self-esteem, mental health, and ability to self-regulate. It is important to help children accept and embrace their emotions. As previously mentioned, an important message to send children is, "Our thoughts and feelings aren't good or bad—they just *are*."

CHAPTER 3
THOUGHTS, FEELINGS, AND BEHAVIORS

All day, every day, different things happen. I have thoughts and feelings about what's happening. I also have different feelings in my body and want to do different things based on what's happening. My thoughts, feelings, and behaviors all affect each other.

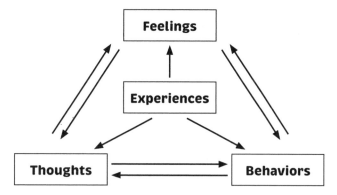

For example, the first time I went off of the diving board at the pool, I felt nervous. I thought, "I can't do this! I'm going to fall!" That thought made me feel more nervous. My heart started beating really fast, my breathing moved from my belly to my chest, and my shoulders got tight. All of those feelings in my body made me even more nervous! I wanted to turn around and get off of the diving board, but I knew I would feel bummed if I didn't try jumping.

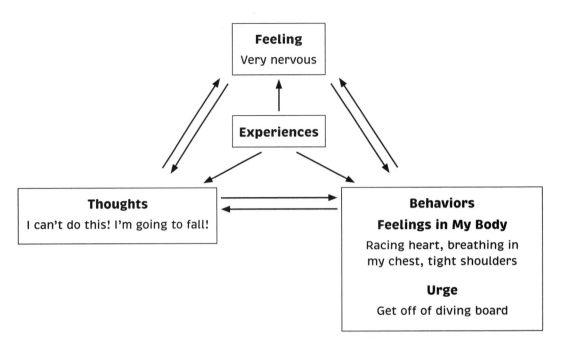

It's helpful to notice what my thoughts are, what my feelings are, and what my behaviors are. I can't control the things that happen, but I can control the ways that I think about them and the things that I do. This gives me the power to deal with whatever feelings and experiences come my way!

When I was on the diving board, I realized that my Automatic Thought was not true and not helpful. I then thought, "I can jump off of the diving board! I can be careful and try not to fall off. If I do fall, I'll probably be okay. There's a lifeguard to make sure I'm safe." That made me feel less nervous. I took some deep breaths and relaxed my shoulders. That made me feel even less nervous. I was then able to take control of my feelings and jump off of the diving board, even though I was nervous. I did it and I was okay! Next time I went to jump off of the diving board, I felt excited instead of nervous.

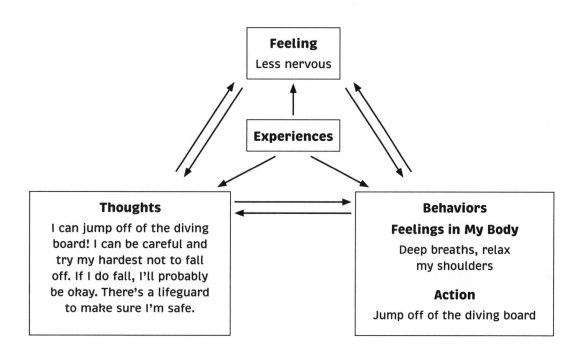

Feeling
Less nervous

Experiences

Thoughts
I can jump off of the diving board! I can be careful and try my hardest not to fall off. If I do fall, I'll probably be okay. There's a lifeguard to make sure I'm safe.

Behaviors
Feelings in My Body
Deep breaths, relax my shoulders

Action
Jump off of the diving board

ACTIVITY

WHAT IS IT—A THOUGHT, A FEELING, OR A BEHAVIOR?

Learning and practicing to notice the difference between thoughts, feelings, and behaviors helps to give us the power to take control of whatever feelings and experiences come our way. Practice doing this by circling if each statement is a thought, feeling, or behavior. *Note: A behavior can either be something that automatically happens in our body or something that we do.*

STATEMENT	CIRCLE ONE		
That's so unfair!	Thought	Feeling	Behavior
I'm crying.	Thought	Feeling	Behavior
I'm jumping for joy.	Thought	Feeling	Behavior
I'm angry.	Thought	Feeling	Behavior
I will never understand the homework.	Thought	Feeling	Behavior
I'm yelling.	Thought	Feeling	Behavior
He's mean.	Thought	Feeling	Behavior
I'm overwhelmed.	Thought	Feeling	Behavior

Answers:

1. Thought, 2. Behavior, 3. Behavior, 4. Feeling, 5. Thought, 6. Behavior 7. Thought, 8. Feeling

◇◇◇◇

NOTE TO THE GROWN-UPS: Differentiating between the emotion of anger and aggressive behavior tends to be particularly challenging for people. It is common in our society to talk and think about anger and aggressive behavior as the same thing. This can lead to children believing that it is bad to experience the feeling of anger. It is important to help children understand that it is normal and healthy to feel angry. We often get the urge to exhibit aggressive behavior when we feel angry, but anger and aggressive behavior are not the same thing. We can feel angry and react in a way that is not aggressive.

ACTIVITY
JUST THE FACTS

Have a grown-up help you pick a video clip that is two minutes or shorter. Try watching it and describe what happens in as many details as possible, but only include the facts. Don't include any feelings, thoughts, or opinions about what is happening. A fact is something that we can all close our eyes and imagine happening in the same way.

Here's an example. I watched the video "Watch This Baby's Hilarious Reaction to First Taste of Ice Cream" by *Good Morning America* on YouTube.

The first time I tried describing it, here is what I wrote:

The baby ate a bite of ice cream. She loved it so much that she grabbed it and was so excited to eat more.

That description is filled with my thoughts and opinions about what happened! I can assume, but I don't really know for sure what the baby is feeling. Here is how I described the video using just the facts:

The baby ate a bite of ice cream. She looked at it. Her eyes got wide. She grabbed it, held it tightly, and continued eating it.

Now you try! Watch a short video clip and describe it using just the facts—no feelings and no opinions. You can write your description here:

_____

_____

_____

_____

_____

_____

_____

_____

_____

Once I started thinking about the difference between my thoughts, feelings, and behaviors, I learned how to:

STOP: Notice and calm down the feelings in my body;

THINK: Think about my thinking and talk back to any unhelpful thoughts;

and

GO: Choose my actions!

◇◇◇◇

CHAPTER 4
THE FEELINGS IN MY BODY

When we have feelings, our bodies respond. Different feelings give us different sensations in our bodies.

When I met my favorite movie star, I got butterflies in my stomach, my heart raced, and I felt energetic and bouncy from my head to my toes. I felt excited.

When my best friend moved far away, my whole body felt heavy and tired, my throat felt tight, and my eyes got teary. I felt sad.

excited

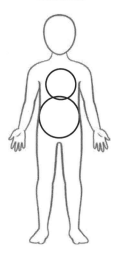

sad

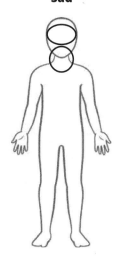

When I was taking pictures with our camera at the zoo and my mom said it was Sammy's turn just as we got to the monkeys, who I really wanted to take pictures of, my face got hot and red, my heart started beating fast, my breathing got short and shallow in my chest, my jaw got tense, and my fists clenched up. I felt angry.

When I heard strange noises in my dark bedroom while I was trying to sleep, my breathing got short and shallow in my chest, my shoulders and jaw got tight and tense, and my heart started racing. I felt nervous.

angry

nervous

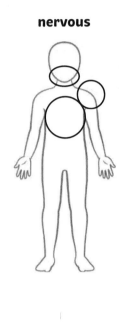

When I notice the feelings in my body, it often helps me realize the emotion that I'm experiencing. This gives me more power to be in control of my emotions and reactions.

ACTIVITY
HOW DOES MY BODY FEEL?

Think about how your body feels when you experience the different emotions. Write and draw to illustrate how the different parts of your body feel for each emotion. It might be helpful to illustrate how your emotions feel as much as possible now and then come back to this activity and add more after you've experienced the emotion, paying attention to what it feels like in your body.

Happy

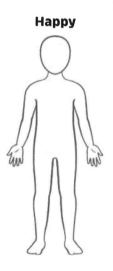

Excited

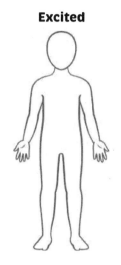

Sad

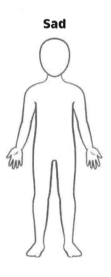

Nervous

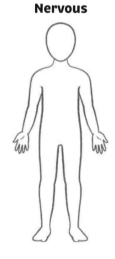

Angry

Embarrassed

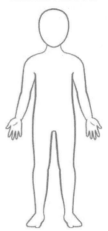

It is normal and can actually be helpful for our bodies to react when we have different feelings. Our feelings all have important jobs. They can help us to spring into action and do something about the situations triggering our feelings.

When I saw a classmate making fun of a new kid at school, I felt sad and angry. Feeling sad and angry motivated me to tell my classmate to leave the new kid alone and to ask the new kid if she wanted to sit with me at lunch.

When I threw a ball and accidentally broke our kitchen window, I felt guilty. Feeling guilty motivated me to apologize to my parents and to be more careful about where I was throwing balls in the future.

When I was competing in a spelling bee, I felt nervous. Feeling nervous motivated me to study and practice before the spelling bee.

Fight, Flight, or Freeze

If you were walking in the jungle and a lion started chasing you, what emotion would you feel?

You would probably feel some shade of threatened or nervous (afraid, anxious, worried, etc.). When we feel threatened or nervous, our bodies react by preparing us for a FIGHT, FLIGHT, or FREEZE reaction. This is helpful when we are actually faced with a threat that we need to protect ourselves from by fighting, running away (flight), or freezing, such as a lion chasing us. When our bodies prepare to fight, our muscles get tense, our breathing gets short and shallow in our chests, and our hearts start beating faster. This gets us ready to punch, kick, or do other fighting actions.

Running also requires our muscles to be tense, our breathing to be short and shallow in our chests, and our hearts to beat faster, so the same things happen in our bodies when they prepare to run away (or flight) from something. Our bodies prepare to freeze in a similar way, but sometimes we hold our breath instead of simply having short, shallow breaths. When our bodies are prepared to fight, flight, or freeze, it sends the message to our heads that we should take one of these actions. That's often unhelpful when we feel nervous, as there usually isn't anything that we actually need to fight, run away from, or freeze to stay hidden from.

We are going to do a physical activity to help us understand the purpose of some of the different feelings we get in our bodies when we experience different emotions. This activity is going to require you to move around, so make sure to choose a good time and location for a little exercise!

ACTIVITY
LOOK OUT FOR THE LION!

Imagine that the lion is chasing you. RUN! Run as fast as you can for two minutes (running in place counts!). After two minutes of running as fast as you can, stop and answer the following questions:

1. Is your heart beating fast or slow?   ❏ Fast   ❏ Slow

2. Is your breathing moving your belly or your chest?   ❏ Belly   ❏ Chest

3. Is your breathing fast or slow?   ❏ Fast   ❏ Slow

4. Were your muscles tight or relaxed?   ❏ Tight   ❏ Relaxed

Usually, when we run as fast as we can, our hearts beat fast, our breathing gets fast, short, and shallow in our chests, and our muscles get tight.

Now imagine that the lion is catching up to you, but there's a bush nearby. Pretend that you jump into the bush. FREEZE! Maybe if you're still, the lion won't see you. Try not to move a muscle for two minutes. After two minutes of freezing, stop and answer the following questions:

1. Is your heart beating fast or slow?   ❏ Fast   ❏ Slow

2. Is your breathing moving your belly or your chest?   ❏ Belly   ❏ Chest

3. Were you holding your breath at all?   ❏ Yes   ❏ No

4. Were your muscles tight or relaxed?   ❏ Tight   ❏ Relaxed

It is common for our hearts to beat fast, our breathing to be short and shallow in our chest or for us to hold our breath, and for our muscles to be tight when we freeze.

Now imagine that the lion found you. It's time to FIGHT!!!! Stand up (far away from other people) and pretend to fight off the lion by kicking and punching the air with all of your strength. Do this for two minutes and then answer the following questions:

1. Is your heart beating fast or slow?   ❏ Fast   ❏ Slow

2. Is your breathing moving your belly or your chest?   ❏ Belly   ❏ Chest

3. Is your breathing fast or slow? ❏ Fast ❏ Slow

4. Were your muscles tight or relaxed? ❏ Tight ❏ Relaxed

When we fight, it is typical for our hearts to beat fast; our breathing to be fast, short, and shallow in our chest; and our muscles to be tight.

◇◇◇◇

ACTIVITY
RATING OUR REACTIONS

Come up with examples of what it might look like if you were to fight, run away (flight), or freeze when faced with the triggers listed. Circle the actions that would be helpful responses to the triggers. Underline the actions that would be unhelpful responses to the triggers.

TRIGGER	FIGHT RESPONSES	FLIGHT RESPONSES	FREEZE RESPONSES
Taking a test	Say something aggressive to the teacher Throw my pencil Punch the desk	Pretend to be sick Hide in the bathroom	Stare at the test and do nothing
Riding your bike			
Going to a party			
Going to the doctor			

When we feel afraid or anxious, it is common to feel it in our bodies like this:

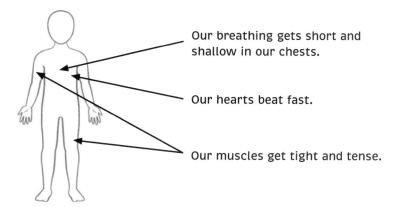

Our breathing gets short and shallow in our chests.

Our hearts beat fast.

Our muscles get tight and tense.

These physical changes in our bodies prepare us for a FIGHT, FLIGHT, or FREEZE response. It is important to be able to fight, run away, or freeze if a lion is chasing us, but it's pretty rare for our anxiety to be triggered by a lion.

When we feel anxious and our bodies get ready for a fight, flight, or freeze response, but there isn't actually any reason to fight, run away, or freeze, the feelings in our bodies can trigger us to feel stronger anxiety.

Remember when I mentioned feeling nervous before competing in a spelling bee? Well, when it was time to go up for my first turn during the spelling bee, my body became filled with worry. My breathing got short and shallow in my chest, my shoulders got tense, and my heart started racing. I wanted to run away. I noticed these sensations in my body and realized that I was feeling an 8 of nervous on the Feelings Thermometer. I relaxed my body. After relaxing my body, the worry didn't go away, but it was less strong. I felt a 3 of nervous on the Feelings Thermometer. Calming down my body sent a message to my head that there was nothing to run away from. This helped me to take control of the worry. I went up for my turn and did the best that I could. I didn't let worry stop me from competing!

When I notice different feelings in my body, it helps me to identify my emotions and sets me up to do something to calm down.

This is the first step to taking control of my feelings.

CHAPTER 5
RELAXATION TECHNIQUES

Relaxing our bodies can help to make the emotions less strong. When our emotions are less strong, we have more power to stay in control of them.

There are different things that we can do to take charge of our bodies. I'll teach you some of my favorite ways to relax my body!

NOTE TO THE GROWN-UPS: Try to make learning and practicing relaxation exercises a fun part of your child's daily routine. The more a child practices these exercises, the more likely they will be able to use them effectively to help manage emotions in the moment. It can be a calm, relaxing experience or it can even be a silly experience. Sometimes a little silliness helps children to remember the tools. There are plenty of opportunities to be silly when practicing these relaxation exercises. As you will see, relaxation involves fingers in belly buttons and clenching our buttocks muscles!

Belly Button Breathing

Find a comfortable position sitting in a chair. Put your finger in your belly button. Notice if your belly is rising and falling with each breath. If it's not, shift your breathing so that it does. Breathe in through your nose for about four seconds and breathe out through your mouth for about five to eight seconds. Do this for two minutes or until you feel calmer.

Toy Breathing

Find a comfortable position lying down. Place a stuffed animal or other small, light toy over your belly button. Watch the toy go up as you breathe in and go down as you breathe out. If the toy is not rising and falling, shift your breathing so that it does.

Continue breathing and watching the toy go up and down with each breath for two minutes or until you feel calmer.

One-Nostril Breathing

Hold one of your nostrils closed with your finger and close your mouth. Slowly breathe in and out through the other nostril. This type of breathing can be especially helpful when you are having difficulty catching your breath.

The Ragdoll Technique

1. Sit on a chair.

2. Make fists and squeeze your hands and arms as tight possible. Keep squeezing them tighter and tighter. Squeeze even tighter as you count to 10. Relax all of your muscles, take a deep breath out, and shake any remaining tension out of your hands and arms. Make them loose and floppy like a ragdoll. Notice the difference between tight and relaxed.

3. Now squeeze your shoulders, lifting them up toward your ears, and tighten your neck. Squeeze as tight as possible. Keep squeezing tighter as you count to 10. Then relax, take a deep breath out, and make your shoulders and neck loose and floppy like a ragdoll. Release all of your muscles, making a wide space between your shoulders and ears.

4. Next, squeeze your bottom muscles. Squeeze them as tight as possible for 10 seconds, take a deep breath out, and release the tension from your bottom.

5. Stretch your legs out in front of you and flex your toes up to the sky. Squeeze as tight as possible and count to 10. Breathe out, relax, drop your legs, release all the muscles, and shake them out.

6. Stretch your legs in front of you again, but this time, point your toes away from you. Squeeze tighter and tighter as you count to 10. Drop your legs to the ground, take a deep breath out, and shake out the tension, making your legs loose and floppy like a ragdoll.

7. Next, tighten up your face muscles. Squeeze your eyes shut, clench your eyebrows and forehead, tighten your nose, and clench your jaw. Squeeze as tight as possible for 10 seconds, and then let it all go. Open your mouth and wiggle your jaw as you completely relax all of your face muscles.

8. Squeeze your whole body as tight as possible. Keep squeezing tighter and tighter as you count to

9. Then, completely relax your body, flopping completely into your chair. Your muscles should be so relaxed that if someone came and picked up your arm, it would flop right back down, just like a floppy ragdoll.

The Chair Technique

Sit in a chair with your feet flat on the ground. Grab underneath the chair with your hands and pull up with all of your strength. Press your feet into the ground and push down with all of your strength. Count to 10 as you continue to pull up with your arms and push down with your feet. When you get to 10, completely relax your muscles. Feel the difference between tense and relaxed. Try to wiggle out any tension that's left over in your body.

Shake and Roll Out the Stress

Shake your hands as if you're trying to dry water off of them. Imagine all of your stress and tension flying out of your fingertips as you continue to shake them as fast as possible for 10 seconds. Drop your hands down by your sides. Your fingers might feel tingly. Take a few deep breaths and notice any relaxed or tingly sensations in your arms and hands. Slowly roll your shoulders forward three times, and then slowly roll your shoulders back three times. Press your shoulders down, making the space between your shoulders and ears as wide as possible. Slowly press your left ear down toward your left shoulder and then press your right ear down toward your right shoulder. Bring your head back to a neutral position.

I like to practice these relaxation exercises every night before I go to bed. This helps me to relax before I sleep. Practicing these exercises at night has also helped me to get better at using them to take control of my feelings in the moment. It used to be hard to remember to use these exercises when I felt angry, upset, anxious, or other uncomfortable feelings. Sometimes I did remember to use them but it felt like they weren't helping me to calm down. The more I practiced relaxation exercises, the better I became at using them to chill out my feelings.

NOTE TO THE GROWN-UPS: It can be helpful to make time to practice relaxation exercises an ongoing part of your child's daily routine. As you and your child are just learning and internalizing the relaxation exercises, some find it most effective to practice the same exercise every day for one week and then switch to another relaxation exercise the following week. This can help your child begin to feel like an expert on each relaxation exercise and can encourage your child to give each exercise a chance, even if it feels funny at first.

ACTIVITY
RELAXATION EXERCISE PRACTICE

Practice at least one of the relaxation exercises every day for at least five minutes. Use the chart to record the day and the relaxation exercise or exercises that you practiced. It can be helpful to schedule a specific time to do this every day.

DAY	RELAXATION EXERCISE(S) PRACTICED

When I notice my mood changing, it helps to stop and do a relaxation exercise to calm down before I react. I like to use different relaxation exercises for different feelings and different situations. I'll share some stories about times when relaxation exercises helped me to deal with strong feelings.

Whenever I go on an airplane, I feel nervous. As soon as I'm seated, I put my finger on my belly button and do Belly Button Breathing until we take off. Belly Button Breathing helps me to make the anxiety I feel while flying a little less strong.

I was so upset when I found out about a birthday party that I wasn't invited to. I wasn't even enjoying playing my favorite video game. I decided to do Toy Breathing. I put a toy car on my stomach and watched it go up and down as I breathed in and out for two minutes. When I was done, I still felt upset, but calmer. I was able to enjoy playing video games more. The feelings eventually passed.

When I accidentally dropped my dad's cell phone in the toilet, I felt so guilty, frustrated with myself, and worried about how he was going to react. I could hardly catch my breath. I did One-Nostril Breathing. Eventually, I was able to catch my breath and deal with the situation.

Sometimes I fight with my sister and my feelings start to take control. When I notice this happening, I tell her that I need a minute, I go to my bedroom, and I do the Ragdoll Technique. Once my body is relaxed, I feel more in control and then I decide if I want to try to deal with whatever Sammy and I were fighting about or let it go and move on with my day.

One day, my teacher called on me to answer a question during class. I gave the wrong answer and heard someone chuckle. I felt so embarrassed and angry. I did the Chair Technique. That helped me to relax my body, which helped me to feel calm and in control, even though I felt embarrassed and angry. The feelings didn't stop me from paying attention and learning. Eventually, the feelings passed.

Doing homework can be stressful. When I notice the stress getting stronger, I take a break to Shake and Roll Out the Stress. This helps to stop my feelings from getting in the way of doing the best that I can on my homework.

These are just some of the many times when relaxation exercises gave me the power to stay in control of my feelings!

It is important to think about where we are and what's going on around us when choosing a relaxation exercise to use. For example, the Ragdoll Technique is not a good relaxation exercise to use when I am sitting in class. It would distract other students from learning, could trigger them to feel confused or annoyed, and they might react in ways that make me feel bad. The Chair Technique or Belly Button Breathing can both be done in a much quieter, less noticeable way. The Ragdoll Technique can be super helpful and more appropriate to use when I'm calming down in the school counselor's office.

ACTIVITY
CHOOSING RELAXATION EXERCISES BY CONSIDERING MY SURROUNDINGS

Think about each setting and write down the different relaxation exercises that you would be helpful for you to use in each one.

In the classroom at school:

_____

_____

In the school counselor's office:

_____

_____

At recess:

_____

_____

At the table when eating dinner with my family:

_____

_____

In my bedroom:

_____

_____

In the car:

_____

_____

Other: _____

_____

_____

ACTIVITY
TAKE CONTROL WITH RELAXATION EXERCISES

Try practicing relaxation exercises to calm down when you're having strong feelings. You can fill out this chart in the moment, which can help you remember to try using the tool. You can also fill out the chart later, after the feelings pass. Thinking about feelings we previously experienced and how we dealt with them can help us to learn from those experiences. Either way of filling out the chart is helpful!

WHAT HAPPENED	HOW I FELT BEFORE (EMOTION AND RATING ON FEELINGS THERMOMETER)	RELAXATION EXERCISE TRIED	HOW I FELT AFTER (EMOTION AND RATING ON FEELINGS THERMOMETER)
Example: I was in the middle of a game. My mom told me to come to dinner.	Annoyed (8)	Belly Button Breathing	Annoyed (4)

WHAT HAPPENED	HOW I FELT BEFORE (EMOTION AND RATING ON FEELINGS THERMOMETER)	RELAXATION EXERCISE TRIED	HOW I FELT AFTER (EMOTION AND RATING ON FEELINGS THERMOMETER)

◇◇◇◇

CHAPTER 6
MY AUTOMATIC THOUGHTS

I used to think that "things that happen" cause my feelings, but I learned that my feelings are shaped by the way I think about those things that happen. I don't always notice my thoughts. Learning how to think about my thinking helped me to take control of my feelings!

I can have totally different feelings about the same thing happening depending on how I think about it. Let me show you what I mean...

One day I woke up, looked out the window, and saw that it was raining. I thought, "Oh good! It's raining! We forgot to water our garden yesterday. Now the plants won't be so thirsty!" I felt happy.

Another time, I woke up, looked out the window, and saw that it was raining. I thought, "Oh no! It's raining! I was supposed to go for a bike ride with my friend today. Now our plan is ruined!" I felt sad.

A few weeks later, I woke up, looked out the window, and saw that it was raining. I thought, "Uh oh! It's raining! Last time it rained I slipped and ripped my favorite pants. I'm totally going to slip again." I felt nervous.

Then there was a time that I woke up, looked out the window, saw that it was raining, and thought, "Oh. It's raining. Bummer. I guess I'll be playing inside today." I felt a little bummed.

On these four different days, the same thing happened: I looked out the window and saw that it was raining. My feelings about the rain were different each day because my Automatic Thoughts were different. Automatic Thoughts are the thoughts or images that pop into our head when something happens.

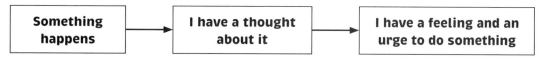

These thoughts make us feel different ways about the things that happen.

ACTIVITY
NAME THE FEELINGS AND THOUGHTS

Read the different scenarios and thoughts. Name the feelings that each thought would trigger and rate how strong they would be on the Feelings Thermometer.

SOMETHING HAPPENS	THOUGHT	FEELING	RATING ON THERMOMETER
I am taking a test.	I am going to fail.		
I am taking a test.	I'll do the best that I can, and that will be good enough.		
My dad said I have to clean my room before playing.	I never get to have any fun!		
My dad said I have to clean my room before playing.	I'll get this over with as quickly as possible, and then I will play.		
It's time to get out of bed and get ready for school.	I don't want to get out of bed! I'm tired. I need to stay in bed!		
It's time to get out of bed and get ready for school.	I don't want to get out of bed, but I can do it. Getting out of bed and going to school will be good for me.		

NOW TRY THIS: Read the different scenarios and come up with a thought that would trigger each of the identified feelings.

SOMETHING HAPPENS	THOUGHT	FEELING	THERMOMETER RATING
I have to get a shot.		Nervous	8
I have to get a shot.		Nervous	2
My sister is singing.		Annoyed	6
My sister is singing.		Entertained	6
I lost a game of checkers.		Upset	5
I lost a game of checkers.		Happy; Upset (Sometimes we can feel more than one way about the same thing at the same time!)	6; 1

◇◇◇◇

Our Automatic Thoughts aren't good or bad—they just *are*. Everyone has Automatic Thoughts that aren't true and aren't helpful sometimes.

When I have thoughts that are unhelpful and untrue, I call them Feelings Monster Thoughts. I like to imagine a little monster in my head saying the unhelpful thought. I know there's not really a monster in my head, but it's easier for me to pretend to talk back to a Feelings Monster than it is to talk back to myself!

NOTE TO THE GROWN-UPS: The Feelings Monster/Feelings Monster Thoughts is a way to help children externalize their feelings. When children are able to see that their feelings are separate from themselves, it supports their ability to identify their thoughts and feelings more accurately, think about situations more objectively, challenge their thoughts, and choose their actions. We can help children understand that even when it seems like feelings are a part of us, they are just something that we have.

ACTIVITY
FEELINGS MONSTER
FINGER PUPPET

You are going to create a Feelings Monster finger puppet. You can use this Feelings Monster finger puppet when you are challenging Feelings Monster Thoughts by putting him on your finger, having him say the thought, and talking back to him.

Follow these instructions to make your Feelings Monster finger puppet:

1. Draw and color a monster in the rectangle provided.

2. With the help of a grown-up, cut out the Feelings Monster attached to the wings.

3. Have a grown-up wrap the wings around your finger so that it is snug but will easily slip on and off of your finger. Secure it in place with glue, blue tack, or tape.

Draw your Feelings Monster In this rectangle:

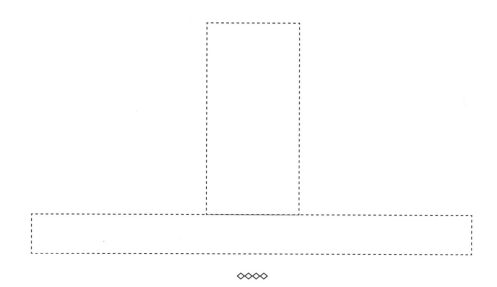

Remember when I was having all of those different thoughts and feelings about the rain? Some of the thoughts I was having were helpful and true. Some of the thoughts I was having were unhelpful and not based on facts.

My thoughts were helpful and true when I saw the rain and thought, "Oh good! It's raining! We forgot to water our garden yesterday. Now the plants won't be so thirsty!"

It was a Feelings Monster Thought when I thought, "Oh no! It's raining! I was supposed to go for a bike ride with my friend today. Now our plan is ruined!" While it's disappointing when plans change, it doesn't mean things are ruined. We could have found something else to do in the rain and planned to ride our bikes another day.

It was also a Feelings Monster Thought when I thought, "Uh oh! It's raining! Last time it rained I slipped and ripped my favorite pants. I'm totally going to slip again." Just because I slipped in the past doesn't mean that I'm going to slip again. Instead of being too nervous to go out in the rain, I can just be a little extra careful and try not to slip when it's raining outside.

I felt bummed when I thought, "Oh. It's raining. Bummer. I guess I'll be playing inside today," but my thought wasn't a Feelings Monster Thought. Sometimes we feel unpleasant emotions even when we're having healthy thoughts that are based on fact. Remember, it's human to experience unpleasant emotions sometimes. They'll pass and there are things we can do to feel less bad even when there are no Feelings Monster Thoughts to challenge.

Having Feelings Monster Thoughts is normal and okay. We can learn how to notice our thoughts, decide if they are helpful or unhelpful, and talk back to them when they're unhelpful!

NOTE TO THE GROWN-UPS: Automatic Thoughts come and go very quickly. They can come in the form of words or images. Most people do not realize when they are having these thoughts. You can help your child learn to identify their Automatic Thoughts by asking, "What were you just thinking?" when you notice that their mood has changed. When feelings are intense, it's difficult for people to identify thoughts and even more difficult to acknowledge when thoughts are unhelpful. It's important to support your child in calming down by using a relaxation exercise, offering a distraction, or giving them time before asking them to think about their thinking.

ACTIVITY
WHAT WERE YOU THINKING?

Think about times when you experienced the following feelings. Write down what happened, what your thought was, and how strong the feeling was on the Feelings Thermometer.

FEELING	WHAT HAPPENED?	THOUGHT	RATING ON FEELINGS THERMOMETER
Sad	My friend told a joke and everyone laughed. I didn't understand the joke.	I'm such a dope. Everyone understands the joke but me.	8
Angry			
Embarrassed			
Nervous			
Frustrated			

◇◇◇◇

Here is a list of some of the most common types of unhelpful Feelings Monster Thoughts, partially adapted from the book *Cognitive Behavior Therapy*, Second Edition, by Judith Beck:

All-or-Nothing Thinking: You see things in black-and-white categories. Things are either good or bad. It has to be one way or you see it as not okay.

Example: If I don't get straight A's on my report card, I'm a total failure.

Overgeneralization: You see a single negative event as a never-ending pattern of defeat. You think this is always going to happen, or this will always be the way it is.

Example: I don't understand the math problem. I'll never get this.

Labeling: This is an extreme form of overgeneralization. Instead of describing your mistake, you see yourself as something negative. When someone else does something that you don't like, you attach a negative label to that person. When we label and mislabel, we describe things with words that are loaded with feelings.

Example: I'm a loser. He's a jerk.

Mental filter: You pick out a negative detail and focus only on that. Like a drop of ink that changes the color of an entire cup of water, this type of thinking darkens the way you see things.

Example: Because I messed up on one step in my performance, it means I had a lousy performance (even though I danced well for the rest of it).

Disqualifying the positive: You think positive things don't count for one reason or another.

Example: I played well in soccer today but that doesn't mean I'm a good soccer player. I just got lucky.

Mind reading: You assume that someone is having negative thoughts about you.

Example: She doesn't want to sit with me at lunch.

The fortune-teller error: You think that things will turn out badly and have feelings as if the bad thing is definitely going to happen. You believe you can't deal with the bad thing if it happens, even if it would just be uncomfortable.

Example: If I sleep over my friend's house, I'm going to get sick. It would be terrible to get sick at a friend's house. I couldn't handle it!

Magnification or Minimization: You blow up the importance of things or shrink things until they seem tiny.

Example: I forgot to do the homework. This is a huge, terrible, awful thing!

Emotional reasoning: You believe something must be true just because you feel that way, even if there are no facts that support your belief.

Example: I have friends and people who want to spend time with me, but I feel like I'm not cool.

"Should" and "must" statements: You think there is a certain way that everyone, including yourself, should do things. You make it a big deal in your head when things don't go the way you think they should.

Example: I should have done better on the test.

Personalization: You blame yourself for something negative that happened or someone's negative behavior, even if it's possible or likely that there's another explanation.

Example: The teacher didn't choose me when I raised my hand because she doesn't like me.

Broken record player thinking: You think about something on repeat that may be true but is not helpful to focus on.

Example: (While playing a game with a friend) My family is moving. My family is moving. My family is moving. My family is moving…

Tunnel vision: You only see the parts of a situation that are bad.

Example: Today was terrible. We had to stay inside for recess, we had a really hard test, I got stuck in traffic on the way home, and I was late for my piano lesson.

ACTIVITY
NAME THE TYPE OF FEELINGS MONSTER THOUGHT

Try to identify the type of Feelings Monster Thought.

THOUGHT	TYPE OF THOUGHT
1. I'm not going to like it!	
2. You're mean.	
3. If I can't have vanilla ice cream, I don't want any dessert at all.	
4. She's never going to want to play with me again.	
5. He should have picked me for his team.	

Answers

1. Fortune-teller error, 2. Labeling, 3. All-or-Nothing Thinking, 4. Overgeneralization, 5. Should statements

◇◇◇◇

NOW TRY THIS: Make up your own examples for each of the different types of Feelings Monster Thoughts.

TYPE OF THOUGHT	EXAMPLE
All-or-Nothing Thinking	
Overgeneralization	
Labeling	
Mental filter	
Disqualifying the positive	
Mind reading	
The fortune-teller error	
Magnification or Minimization	
Emotional reasoning	
"Should" and "must" statements	
Personalization	
Broken record player thinking	
Tunnel vision	

◇◇◇◇

I have thousands of thoughts every day. I don't always notice the thoughts bopping around in the back of my head, but I learned how to stop and think about my thinking when my mood changed. Trying to notice the types of thoughts that I sometimes have helped me to identify when my thoughts were unhelpful. Let me tell you about a few times when I noticed my unhelpful thoughts.

One day, my mom told me to study for a science test. I started crying and repeating that I didn't want to study. My mom asked me to go to my room to calm down for a few minutes. She came to my room and asked, "What was going through your mind when I said it was time to study?" I thought about my thinking and said, "This test is going to be really hard. I don't understand this stuff and I'm going to fail the test no matter what." When I was calmer, I was able to see that I was having Feelings Monster Thoughts. I was having fortune teller error and overgeneralization thoughts. Just noticing that helped me to move on and study.

WHAT HAPPENED?	THOUGHT	FEELINGS	RATINGS ON FEELINGS THERMOMETER
My mom told me to study for the science test.	This test is going to be really hard. I don't understand this stuff, and I'm going to fail the test no matter what.	Nervous	8
		Frustrated	6
		Hopeless	8
		Insecure	7

Another time, the fire alarm started going off in school. I suddenly had lots of big feelings. I asked myself, "What am I thinking right now?" I realized that my thought was, "It's too loud. I can't handle this!" I noticed it was a Feelings Monster Thought: magnification. I was blowing up the power that the alarm has over me. The fire alarm is really loud, but I've handled it before and knew it would stop soon. Just being aware of the Feelings Monster Thought helped me to feel a little less bad.

WHAT HAPPENED?	THOUGHT	FEELINGS	RATINGS ON FEELINGS THERMOMETER
The fire alarm went off in school.	It's too loud. I can't handle this!	Annoyed	9
		Overwhelmed	8

NOTE TO THE GROWN-UPS: Try to notice patterns in the types of unhelpful thoughts that your child has. Automatic Thoughts can be somewhat predictable. When your child has intense feelings, you can validate her feelings and then say something to challenge what you predict she is thinking. For example, Alex's mother in the above scenario about studying could say, "The idea of studying for this test is overwhelming, but you can do it. Studying will set you up to do the best that you can on this test. Whatever your best is will be good enough."

Parents have feelings too, so it's very possible that Alex's mother may have had the urge to yell at Alex for his behavior. Validating Alex's feelings and proactively trying to challenge what she predicted Alex was thinking would have been more likely to get her desired results: for Alex to calm down and study. In the other example, when the fire alarm went off in school, the teacher could have predicted that it might trigger some children, so he could say, "The fire alarm is going off but we're all okay. We are going to quickly and quietly line up and go where we need to go. This will be over soon."

ACTIVITY
CATCHING MY THOUGHTS

For one week, try to catch yourself having at least three Feelings Monster Thoughts. Write down what happened, what your thought was, the feeling, and the rating of the feeling on the Feelings Thermometer. You can try to do this in the moment when you're having the feelings or later when you're thinking about the feelings you had that day.

WHAT HAPPENED?	THOUGHT	FEELING	RATING ON FEELINGS THERMOMETER

◇◇◇◇

CHAPTER 7
TAKING CONTROL OF MY THOUGHTS

Once I learned how to notice my thoughts and decide if they are helpful or unhelpful, then I learned how to talk back to them. Talking back to unhelpful thoughts can make my feelings less strong and help me to stay in control of how I react. I'll teach you some tools that help me to talk back to my thoughts.

NOTE TO THE GROWN-UPS: Assess how intense your child's emotions are before trying to help them challenge their thoughts. When a child's emotions are intense, they will not have the ability to use their executive functions effectively, and thus will have extreme difficulty evaluating their thinking. You can encourage your child to use a relaxation exercise or do something else to calm down until the intensity of their emotions has decreased and they are in a better mindset to identify and challenge their unhelpful thoughts.

One day, I decided to try to learn a trick on my skateboard. I tried a few times and kept falling. I thought, "I can't do anything right. I never should have tried this." I felt really sad and insecure. I went to my bedroom and decided to fill out the Thought Challenge Worksheet to try to make myself feel less bad. The Thought Challenge Worksheet asks me questions that help me to notice and challenge Feelings Monster Thoughts. Here is the worksheet—which is partially adapted from *Cognitive Behavior: Basics and Beyond*—by Judith Beck, and my responses:

Thought Challenge Worksheet

1. What's happening (just the facts... no thoughts or opinions about it)?

I tried to learn a new trick on the skateboard and fell several times.

2. What am I thinking about it?

"I can't do anything right. I never should have tried."

3. Is there any evidence that this thought is true?

I tried to do the trick and failed so many times.

4. Is there any evidence that this thought might not be true?

I've done other things right before, including some things that I couldn't do when I first tried.

5. How can I think about this differently?

I might not be able to do it yet, but if I keep trying, I might get it. If I don't get it, I'll survive. There are lots of other things that I'm good at doing.

6. What's the worst thing that could happen? If that happened, how could I deal with it?

Someone might see me messing up the trick and think I'm a loser. I could try to ignore them and remind myself that I'm not a loser. Not being able to do one skateboard trick doesn't define me. Other people's words don't define me either.

7. How could this be a good thing or lead to a good thing?

I could master the trick.

8. What is most likely to happen?

I'll probably figure out how to do it if I keep trying. Even if I don't, other people probably won't judge me for that. If they do, that says more about them than it does about me.

After I filled out the Thought Challenge Worksheet, I felt less sad and insecure. I took a break from skateboarding that day, but I tried again another day and was eventually able to do the trick. I felt so proud!

ACTIVITY
THOUGHT CHALLENGE
WORKSHEET

Read the story. Try filling out the Thought Challenge Worksheet as if you are the character.

I was thinking about trying out for the basketball team. I thought, "I probably won't make the team. What if I mess up during the tryout and everyone laughs at me?" I felt really insecure and considered not trying out.

1. What's happening (just the facts… no thoughts or opinions about it)?

_____

_____

2. What am I thinking about it?

_____

_____

3. Is there any evidence that this thought is true?

_____

_____

4. Is there any evidence that this thought might not be true?

_____

_____

5. How can I think about this differently?

_____

_____

6. What's the worst that could happen? If that happened, how could I deal with it?

_____

_____

7. How could this be a good thing or lead to a good thing?

_____

_____

8. What is most likely to happen?

_____

_____

NOW TRY THIS: Fill out the Thought Challenge Worksheet for one of your real-life situations.

1. What's happening (just the facts... no thoughts or opinions about it)?

_____

_____

_____

_____

_____

2. What am I thinking about it?

_____

_____

_____

_____

3. Is there any evidence that this thought is true?

_____

_____

_____

_____

_____

4. Is there any evidence that this thought might not be true?

_____

_____

_____

_____

5. How can I think about this differently?

_____

_____

_____

_____

6. What's the worst that could happen? If that happened, how could I deal with it?

_____

_____

_____

_____

7. How could this be a good thing or lead to a good thing?

_____

_____

_____

_____

_____

8. What is most likely to happen?

_____

_____

_____

_____

_____

Now think about the following:

Did filling out the worksheet change your feelings at all?

_____

_____

_____

_____

Did filling out the worksheet change what your actions would be?

_____

_____

_____

_____

_____

◇◇◇◇

The Thought Challenge Worksheet can help us to think about things in a healthier way, make our feelings less strong, and stay in control of our reactions! You can try using this worksheet any time that it might be helpful. Sometimes I fill out the worksheet when I am having strong feelings. This helps me to take control of my thoughts and feelings in the moment. Sometimes I fill out the worksheet after I've had a strong feeling to help me learn, grow, and move on from the experience.

Thought Records can also help me to notice and talk back to unhelpful thoughts. They can be used in the moment when I'm experiencing the feelings or later on when reflecting about the experience. I'll tell you about a time a Thought Record helped me to take control of my thoughts, feelings, and reactions.

When I walked into the courtyard on my first day at a new school, I saw kids talking and hanging out with each other. I thought, "I'm never going to make friends here. Everyone already has their groups. Nobody is going to want to hang out with me." I felt really sad, lonely, and nervous. While I did meet some kids who seemed nice throughout the day, the thoughts and feelings didn't go away. When I got home, I decided to do a Thought Record. Here it is:

1. SOMETHING HAPPENS		
I started going to a new school.		
2. AUTOMATIC THOUGHTS (OPTIONAL: IDENTIFY TYPE OF THOUGHT)		3. FEELINGS AND RATING ON FEELINGS THERMOMETER
I'm never going to make friends here. Everyone already has their groups. Nobody is going to want to hang out with me. (Fortune teller error, Mind reading)		Sad (8) Lonely (9)
4. CHALLENGE THOUGHT		5. FEELINGS AND RATING ON FEELINGS THERMOMETER
I will probably make friends here. They might know each other and have friends already, but that doesn't mean they won't want to be my friend too.		Sad (3) Lonely (5)

In column 1, "Something happens," I wrote down just the facts about what happened. Describing what happens in a factual way means that others would see it the same way. It's easy to accidentally write feelings, thoughts, and opinions here. For example, I might have wanted to write, "Everyone was talking to a friend except for me."

That's not a fact. That's what I assumed when I walked into the courtyard on that first day of school, but I didn't actually see what everyone was doing.

Those assumptions belong in column 2, "Automatic Thoughts." Automatic Thoughts can be anything that popped into my mind. Sometimes I have a lot of thoughts to write in column 2. It takes up more than one page! Sometimes my Automatic Thoughts are actually an image, which I just describe in words. All of that is okay! Our thoughts are what they are.

In column 3, "Feelings and Rating on Feelings Thermometer," I can list and rate all of the feelings I was experiencing. This might include lots of feelings and can even include conflicting feelings. For example, sometimes I feel both excited and nervous about the same thing.

In column 4, I wrote down a Challenge Thought. A Challenge Thought is something we can say to talk back to an unhelpful thought. It is important for these thoughts to directly talk back to the parts of my Feelings Monster Thoughts that are unhelpful and for them to be believable. Challenge Thoughts usually make me experience the feelings less strongly. I checked if my feelings got any less strong based on the new thought and recorded the new feelings in column 5.

NOTE TO THE GROWN-UPS: It is important for Challenge Thoughts to be realistic and believable. We might feel inclined to "put on rose-colored glasses" and be overly optimistic, but these types of Challenge Thoughts only temporarily help children feel better and sometimes have no soothing effect at all. For example, in this scenario, saying, "Everything is going to be awesome at your new school! You are going to make a ton of friends and be so popular!" could actually trigger a child to feel worse because it's setting the child up for disappointment in the likely scenario that everything isn't instantly and totally awesome. It's a process to adjust to the new social scene.

Coming up with Challenge Thoughts can be tricky. It's hard to challenge my own thoughts! My feelings make them seem very true, even when they're not. That's why I like to imagine that little Feelings Monster saying the thoughts to me, so I can imagine talking back to the monster. It's easier to talk back to a Feelings Monster than it is to talk back to my own thoughts!

NOTE TO THE GROWN-UPS: It is important to normalize to children that it is challenging to identify and challenge unhelpful thoughts, and to stay in control of feelings in general. Completing these exercises in a workbook about made-up thoughts, feelings, and experiences is much easier than applying them to our real-life thoughts, feelings, and experiences. If a child believes that they should be able to do this right away, they might feel frustration, guilt, shame, or other feelings when it is difficult for them, which will only intensify their emotions and make them more challenging to manage.

ACTIVITY
TALK BACK TO THE FEELINGS MONSTER

Read the scenario. Below, you will see a Feelings Monster saying unhelpful thoughts about the scenario. Practice talking back to the Feelings Monster by filling in the speech bubble with a healthier way of thinking that's more based on reality.

My friend told me about a movie that sounded cool. I really wanted to watch it, but my parents said that I can't see it until I'm older.

Your friend is going to think you're a baby because you couldn't see it!

You'll never get to see this or any other cool movies!

◇◇◇◇

Talking back to thoughts is harder than it sounds. It's easier to talk back to someone else's thoughts. That's because our feelings make our own thoughts seem true, even when they're not. It can be helpful to talk to an adult about your unhelpful thoughts so they can help you to challenge them. I'll tell you about a time when it was really helpful to have an adult help me challenge my thoughts.

NOTE TO THE GROWN-UPS: It is important to validate your child's emotions before diving into challenging their thoughts. If a child feels invalidated, it will exacerbate their level of distress, which will make it more difficult to challenge their thoughts and stay in control of their behavior. Simply saying, "That was really frustrating for you!" can help a child begin to de-escalate, which will set them up to be better able to use the tools to cope with their feelings in a healthy manner. As you support your child in evaluating their thoughts, be sure to avoid evaluating their emotions. Emotions generally make sense once we understand the thoughts shaping them. Thoughts can be irrational and require challenging. Emotions are what they are, and they require validation.

One day, my teacher yelled at me when I was talking during class. I know I'm not supposed to talk during class, but she didn't yell at the other kids when they were talking. I felt angry and hurt. I noticed that I was thinking, "She only yells at me when other kids talk during class too. She likes all of the other kids better than she likes me." I tried to talk back to these thoughts but I felt certain that they were true and could not be challenged. My feelings were so strong that they made it hard to think about the situation in any other way. I was cranky when I came home from school and my dad asked me what was wrong. When I told him what happened and what I was thinking, he told me that he understood how bad it made me feel when the teacher yelled at me. He then helped me consider some other ways to think about the situation. Here is the Thought Record that we filled out together:

1. SOMETHING HAPPENS	
The teacher yelled at me when I was talking. She didn't yell at other kids when they were talking.	

2. AUTOMATIC THOUGHTS (OPTIONAL: IDENTIFY TYPE OF THOUGHT)	3. FEELINGS AND RATING ON FEELINGS THERMOMETER
She only yells at me when other kids talk during class too. She likes all of the other kids better than she likes me. (Overgeneralization, Mind reading)	Angry (8) Hurt (7)

4. CHALLENGE THOUGHT	5. FEELINGS AND RATING ON FEELINGS THERMOMETER
I would prefer it if my teacher reacted the same to all students all of the time, but she's human so that would be hard for her to do. It's possible that I was being more disruptive or the teacher didn't notice the other kids when they were talking. There have been other times when she's yelled at other kids for talking during class. Yelling at me in the moment for breaking a classroom rule does not mean that my teacher does not like me.	Annoyed (3) Hurt (1) Understanding (5)

It helped to talk about the situation with my dad. First, he made me feel understood. Then, he helped me to be able to think about the situation in different ways that were hard to realize on my own when I was feeling so hurt and angry. After our chat, I felt much better and moved on with my day.

ACTIVITY
THOUGHT RECORDS

Read the story. Fill out the Thought Record as if you are the character.

My friends invited me to meet up with them at the park. When I arrived, they were in the middle of a game of tetherball. I tried to get their attention but they simply said, "Hi," and kept playing their game. I thought, "They don't care about me. I shouldn't have come." I felt really sad.

1. SOMETHING HAPPENS	
2. AUTOMATIC THOUGHTS (OPTIONAL: IDENTIFY TYPE OF THOUGHT)	**3. FEELINGS AND RATING ON FEELINGS THERMOMETER**
4. CHALLENGE THOUGHT	**5. FEELINGS AND RATING ON FEELINGS THERMOMETER**

NOW TRY THIS: Fill out a Thought Record for one of your real-life situations. You can do this about a situation that you are dealing with in the moment or you can do this to reflect on a situation that happened in the past. When using a Thought Record to cope with a situation you are dealing with in the moment, try noticing your thoughts and writing them down as soon as you notice your mood getting worse.

1. SOMETHING HAPPENS	
2. AUTOMATIC THOUGHTS (OPTIONAL: IDENTIFY TYPE OF THOUGHT)	**3. FEELINGS AND RATING ON FEELINGS THERMOMETER**
4. CHALLENGE THOUGHT	**5. FEELINGS AND RATING ON FEELINGS THERMOMETER**

Now think about the following:

- Did filling out the Thought Record change your feelings at all?

_____

_____

_____

_____

● Did filling out the Thought Record change what your actions would be?

_____

_____

_____

_____

_____

◇◇◇◇

The more I practiced filling out Thought Records, the better I got at using them to deal with my feelings. After doing a lot of Thought Records, I started noticing that I have some of the same unhelpful thoughts again and again. I call these Repeat Offender Thoughts. When I notice my Repeat Offender Thoughts, I come up with Challenge Thoughts for them. I call these helpful self-statements. I find different ways to think about the helpful self-statements regularly so that I can train my brain to replace my Repeat Offender Thoughts.

Recently, I noticed that I've been thinking, "I'll never be able to do it" about a lot of different things. I thought it when my homework was hard, I thought it when I was learning how to play a new song on the guitar, and I thought it when I was told to clean my very messy bedroom. "I'll never be able to do it" was a Repeat Offender Thought! I came up with the Challenge Thought, "I can try my hardest, do the best that I can, and that's good enough." I wrote this helpful self-statement down on a piece of construction paper, decorated it, and hung it in my bedroom. I also wrote it down on a notecard, which I kept in my pocket when I went to school. Every morning when I woke up and every night before I went to bed, I looked at myself in the mirror and said, "I can try my hardest, do the best that I can, and that's good enough." I haven't stopped sometimes thinking, "I'll never be able to do it," but when I notice that thought, I remember this helpful self-statement. This helps me to take control of my thinking, feelings, and reactions more often and more quickly.

ACTIVITY
HELPFUL SELF-STATEMENTS

On page 96 are helpful self-statements that challenge some common unhelpful thoughts that people have. Decorate each helpful self-statement and cut them out of this workbook. Decide which thoughts are helpful for you. You can read them every day. You can put them somewhere that you'll see them regularly. You can punch a hole in the corner of each one and put them on a binder ring. You can keep them in your pocket to have as a reminder when you are doing something that triggers you. You can look at them to help yourself calm down when you are having big feelings. There are lots of ways that these helpful self-statements can be used to help you take control of your thinking, feelings, and reactions!

HELPFUL SELF-STATEMENTS

This feeling will pass. This stress will pass. I will be okay.

I'm having big feelings right now, but I'm okay.

I can cope with this.

I can hang in there.

Breathe.

I am strong.

My feelings are normal, and they are okay.

Mistakes are opportunities to learn and grow.

I do not have to be perfect.

I have the power to make good choices.

I can't control what other people do, but I can control the way that I think about it and the way that I react to it.

I can have a big feeling and be calm and in control at the same time.

NOW TRY THIS: Think about the unhelpful thoughts that you've had. Have you noticed any Repeat Offender Thoughts? You can look through old Thought Records to try to find thoughts that seem similar to each other. Come up with helpful self-statements that challenge your Repeat Offender Thoughts. Write them in the boxes below, decorate them, and cut them out of this workbook.

Sometimes I have unhelpful thoughts that make me feel bad about myself. When I make a mistake, I think "I'm so stupid!" But everyone makes mistakes! Making a mistake does not make me a stupid person. When I compare myself to other kids, I think, "I'm such a loser!" But I'm not really a loser. Other kids have things that make them cool, and I have things that make me cool. These thoughts are unhelpful Feelings Monster Thoughts that are not based on reality. Let's do an activity to help challenge this type of unhelpful Feelings Monster Thought!

NOTE TO THE GROWN-UPS: When pointing out a child's strengths, it is important to be specific and genuine for it to have a meaningful effect on a child's self-esteem.

ACTIVITY
FEEL-GOOD FILE

A Feel-Good File is a place to collect things that remind us of our positive qualities and strengths. All people have things that make them awesome. Sometimes our unhelpful Feelings Monster Thoughts make it hard to remember our strengths. Creating and looking at our Feel-Good File can help us to combat these negative thoughts.

Materials

- Manila envelope (or any folder or envelope that can hold everything)
- Scissors
- Notecards
- Markers

Instructions

1. Decorate the envelope or folder that you will use as your Feel-Good File.

2. Complete the What I Like About Me worksheet on page 102. Cut the What I Like About Me worksheet out of this book and place it in your Feel-Good File.

3. Cut the three Feel-Good Note worksheets (pages 102-104) out of this book. Ask three different people to complete the notes about you. You can ask anyone you choose: family members, teachers, friends, coaches, or anyone else in your life who makes you feel good about yourself. Put the completed "Feel-Good Notes" in your Feel-Good File.

4. Think about memories of times when you felt good about yourself. This can include your accomplishments, words that people said to you, such as those recognizing your talents or expressing appreciation for you, or any other moments that made you feel good. Write each memory down on a notecard. Place the notecards in your Feel-Good File.

5. Collect items that remind you of your positive qualities and accomplishments you're proud of. Place them in the Feel-Good File. This can include cards you've received, pictures or notes that remind you of positive conversations or experiences,

assignments you're proud of, or anything else that makes you feel proud and good about yourself.

6. Look through your Feel-Good File whenever you want to—especially to help combat unhelpful Feelings Monster Thoughts that make you feel bad!

What I Like About Me...

_____

_____

_____

_____

_____

_____

Feel-Good Note from _____
(Name of person completing note)

When I think of _____,
(Name of Feel-Good File maker)

Five positive qualities that I think about are:

1. _____

2. _____

3. _____

4. _____

5. _____

Feel-Good Note from _____

(Name of person completing note)

When I think of _____,

(Name of Feel-Good File maker)

Five positive qualities that I think about are:

1. _____

2. _____

3. _____

4. _____

5. _____

Feel-Good Note from _____
(Name of person completing note)

When I think of _____,
(Name of Feel-Good File maker)

Five positive qualities that I think about are:

1. _____

2. _____

3. _____

4. _____

5. _____

◇◇◇◇

A lot of unhelpful Feelings Monster Thoughts are not actually about what's happening in the moment. Sometimes when something happens, it makes me have thoughts and feelings about things that have happened in the past or things that I think might happen in the future. People have enough to deal with in the moment—it's too much to have feelings about the past and feelings about something that might never even happen at the same time! Let me tell you about a time that I had these thoughts and a way I took control of them.

My class was going on a field trip, and I felt really anxious about the long bus ride. When we got on the bus, it was hot, loud, and uncomfortable. I thought, "What if I get sick on the bus?" I started imagining getting super-sick and having feelings as if that was definitely going to happen. Then, I started thinking about a time in the past when I did get sick on a bus. I started having feelings about that memory. I was having feelings about the possible future and the past, which was making my anxiety even stronger and making it harder to deal with the moment. I took a deep breath and did the 5, 4, 3, 2, 1 exercise to bring my mind to the moment:

- I named 5 things I could see: 1. My friend, 2. The bus driver, 3. My teacher, 4. My sneakers, 5. The seat in front of me

- I named 4 things I could touch and actually touched them: 1. My backpack, 2. The seat in front of me, 3. The fidget spinner in my pocket, 4. My water bottle

- I named 3 things I could hear: 1. My classmates talking, 2. The sound of the other cars on the road, 3. The air conditioner on the bus

- I named 2 things I could smell and actually smelled them: 1. My shirt, 2. My hand sanitizer

- I noticed what my mouth tasted like

Doing the 5, 4, 3, 2, 1 helped me bring my thinking to just that moment instead of also thinking about the past and the future. I realized that I was okay right now and felt less anxious.

ACTIVITY
5, 4, 3, 2, 1

Sometimes unhelpful Feelings Monster Thoughts trigger us to have feelings about things that happened in the past, things we think might happen in the future, or things we think could be happening but have no evidence that they are. When this happens, we spend a lot of energy having feelings about things that aren't actually happening, which makes our feelings stronger and harder to take control of. Doing the 5, 4, 3, 2, 1 can help us to bring our thoughts to what's actually happening in the moment.

Play this game when you're calm. It's fun, and it can also help you to be able to use it to take control of your unhelpful thoughts in the future! Try using this game to help stay in control of unhelpful Feelings Monster Thoughts that make you have feelings about things that aren't actually happening in the moment.

5. Name 5 things that you can see.

4. Name 4 things that you can touch. Actually touch them.

3. Name 3 things that you can hear (outside of your head- no thoughts!).

2. Name 2 things that you can smell. Actually smell them.

1. Notice what your mouth tastes like.

Sometimes it's hard to stop thinking about something that makes me feel bad. For example, when I failed a test, I kept thinking, "I failed the test" over and over. It was true, but it was not helpful to think about on repeat. This ongoing thought made it hard to focus in school the rest of the day, got in the way of my ability to enjoy anything, and made it hard to fall asleep. Eventually, I realized that it was unhelpful to have this thought on repeat and I took control by looking through my Instant Mood Shifter File! This helped me to shift my thinking to shift my mood, which helped me to move on.

◇◇◇◇

ACTIVITY
INSTANT MOOD SHIFTER FILE

When it's hard to stop thinking about something, it can make us feel even more upset and stressed. Even when a thought is true, it's not helpful to think about it all the time! That just gets in the way of our ability to enjoy the things that are going right. An Instant Mood Shifter File is a place to store images that make you feel happy and relaxed. You can look through the Instant Mood Shifter File when you want to take a break from unhelpful Automatic Thoughts.

Materials

- Manila envelope (or other folder where you can store things)
- Anything that you can fit into your Instant Mood Shifter File that brings you joy! Here are some ideas:

  o Photographs of favorite memories, loved ones, or places

  o Cut-out pictures from magazines of things that you like, such as animals, nature, art, or sports

  o Poems, quotes, or lyrics from favorite songs on notecards

Instructions

1. Decorate your Instant Mood Shifter File.

2. Fill it with as many things that bring you joy as you can think of!

3. Look through your Instant Mood Shifter File whenever you want to—especially to help combat unhelpful Feelings Monster Thoughts that get in the way of experiencing the here and now of your life!

Sometimes it's helpful to simply take a break from our thoughts and feelings. Distractions and the relaxation exercises that we learned earlier in this workbook can help us to take a break from focusing on stressful thoughts, feelings, and situations. Let's learn how we can actually use our thinking to help us relax in these moments too!

◇◇◇◇

ACTIVITY
MENTAL VACATION

Sometimes, it helps to take a break from our thoughts. Taking a Mental Vacation can help us to chill out our thoughts and feelings.

Find a relaxed position, either sitting up or lying down. Close your eyes. Take some deep, relaxing breaths in through your nose and out through your mouth. Make sure that your belly is rising and falling with each breath. Once your body and breathing are relaxed, begin to think of a place where you've actually been that makes you feel calm and relaxed. This can be anywhere. A beach, a bench in the park, your bedroom, a favorite store... anywhere! Begin to imagine this place in as many details as possible. What do you see? What do you smell? What do you hear? Do you taste anything? What's the temperature like? What else do you feel? Imagine doing what you enjoy doing in this relaxing place in as many details as possible. Continue to breathe slowly and deeply as you take a mental vacation to your special place. Know that you can return here in your mind any time that you choose, which can help you to feel calm and relaxed. When you are ready, bring your awareness back to the moment. Notice the feeling of the surface underneath your body where you are sitting or lying down. Start to wiggle your fingers and toes. Open your eyes and return from your mental vacation, bringing your awareness back to the moment.

Once you are feeling calmer and more in control, you can choose how you want to deal with the situation that was triggering your feelings.

Learning to notice and challenge Feelings Monster Thoughts gives me the power to stay in control and deal with whatever feelings and situations come my way!

◇◇◇◇

CHAPTER 8
MY URGES

Whenever I am faced with a trigger and have a feeling, I have an urge to do something. An urge is something that we want to do.

- When I found out we were having a snow day from school, I felt happy and had the urge to smile.

- When I lost a contest that I worked really hard on, I felt sad and had the urge to cry.

- When I was about to go on a really cool ride, I felt excited and had the urge to cheer.

- When my sister spilled juice all over my favorite shirt, I felt angry and had the urge to yell.

- When I saw a huge spider in my bedroom, I felt afraid and had the urge to avoid going in my bedroom.

ACTIVITY
MY URGES

What urges have you had when experiencing each of these feelings? List as many urges as you can think of. Circle the urges that you have most often when experiencing each feeling.

FEELING	URGES
Happy	
Excited	
Proud	
Nervous	
Angry	
Sad	
Embarrassed	

◇◇◇◇

THE SELF-REGULATION WORKBOOK FOR KIDS

I used to feel like I had to act on my urges, but I learned that I have the power to choose my actions. Everything I do is a choice, and every choice I make causes something to happen. Even the little things that I usually don't think about are choices.

When I had an itch on my knee, I made the choice to scratch it. That caused the itch to go away.

When I woke up early on a Saturday morning, I chose to read a comic book. That caused me to feel happy and relaxed.

When I came inside after running around, I chose to drink a big glass of water. That caused me to feel refreshed.

NOTE TO THE GROWN-UPS: Help increase your child's awareness of their ability to make good choices by pointing out the positive choices that you observe them making. For example, you can say, "I love how you just made the choice to ask for help when your work got hard," and "You're disappointed that we don't have any ice cream, and you're choosing to move on and eat cookies instead." Additionally, you can make it a routine for both you and your child to identify at least one positive choice that the child made each day. Some families enjoy doing this during dinner or as part of the bedtime routine. This can help your child build confidence and awareness that will support their ability to make good choices.

ACTIVITY
WHAT DO MY CHOICES CAUSE?

Read the choices and list what each choice is likely to cause.

CHOICE	WHAT IT COULD CAUSE
Example: Brushing my teeth	• My breath will smell good • I'll be less likely to get cavities
Giving my friend a compliment	
Saying, "I'm sorry" after making a mistake	
Picking up litter in the park	
Throwing a tantrum	
Laughing at a classmate for making a mistake	
Giving up when something gets hard	

NOW TRY THIS: Think of choices that you made in the past week and what they caused. Write them on the chart.

CHOICE MADE	WHAT IT CAUSED

◇◇◇◇

Acting on my urges often feels good in the moment, but it causes things that make me feel worse later. Something that makes me feel good in the moment is called instant gratification. Something that makes me feel good later is called delayed gratification. It is helpful to think about what my choices will cause in the moment and what my choices will cause later before choosing my actions.

One night, my parents told me that it was time to go to bed because I had to be up early for school the next day, but I didn't want to. I snuck a flashlight into my bedroom and stayed up all night reading under the covers. I really liked the book, and it felt exciting to secretly stay up all night. The next day, I regretted this choice. I was tired and cranky all day. Even little things annoyed me. It was really hard to focus all day, which was especially stressful when it was time to take a math test. I did not do as well as I could have on my math test. I made the choice to stay up all night because it made me feel happy in the moment.

This is an example of instant gratification. The negative things that this choice caused ended up making me feel bad in ways that lasted longer than the positive feelings I experienced from staying up all night.

CHOICE	WHAT IT CAUSED IN THE MOMENT	WHAT IT CAUSED LATER
Staying up all night and reading under my covers	I felt happy I felt excited I enjoyed the book	I felt tired I felt cranky I had trouble focusing I did not do well on a math test

ACTIVITY
WHAT CHOICES CAUSE NOW AND LATER

Read the triggers and choices, and complete the choice charts. Circle the things it caused that would make a bigger difference and last longer.

Trigger: I feel bored during class.

CHOICE	WHAT IT COULD CAUSE IN THE MOMENT	WHAT IT COULD CAUSE LATER
Write a note and pass it to my friend.		

Trigger: I want to use a blue marker during art class, but they are all being used by other students.

CHOICE	WHAT IT COULD CAUSE IN THE MOMENT	WHAT IT COULD CAUSE LATER
Use a green marker while I wait for my turn with a blue marker.		

NOW TRY THIS: Think about three choices that you made this week. Write down the trigger, the choice, what each choice caused in the moment, and what each choice caused later. Circle the things it caused that made a bigger difference and lasted longer.

Trigger: _____

CHOICE	WHAT IT COULD CAUSE IN THE MOMENT	WHAT IT COULD CAUSE LATER

Trigger: _____

CHOICE	WHAT IT COULD CAUSE IN THE MOMENT	WHAT IT COULD CAUSE LATER

Trigger: _____

CHOICE	WHAT IT COULD CAUSE IN THE MOMENT	WHAT IT COULD CAUSE LATER

◇◇◇◇

Sometimes it feels like I have to act on my urges, but I can have a feeling and an urge and choose not to act on it. We'll learn more about how to have an urge and stay in control later. My feelings are stronger and my urges are harder to stay in control of whenever I am HUNGRY, ANGRY, LONELY, or TIRED. "Halt" is another word for "stop." HALT can also stand for Hungry, Angry, Lonely, and Tired. When I start to notice my feelings getting stronger, I always remember to HALT, or STOP! Then I ask myself if I am:

- Hungry

- Angry

- Lonely

- Tired

If I notice that I am any of these things, I try to solve that before choosing my actions.

- If I am hungry, I eat something.

- If I am angry, I do something to try to deal with the feeling, such as a relaxation exercise or talking to someone about my feelings.

- If I am lonely, I spend time with another person.

- If I am tired, I sleep.

My family planned on watching a movie together one night, but my mom had to finish some work first. It felt like she was taking forever. I started feeling really impatient and frustrated. When I noticed my feelings getting stronger, I HALTed. I asked myself, "Am I hungry? Am I angry? Am I lonely? Am I tired?" I noticed that I was feeling both hungry and lonely. I ate a snack and then went to hang out with my sister while I waited for everyone to be ready to watch the movie. Noticing and doing something about the fact that I was hungry and lonely helped to make my feelings of impatience and frustration a little less strong and easier to deal with.

NOTE TO THE GROWN-UPS: Make sure that your child stays hydrated and eats a balanced diet of protein, fats, and especially carbohydrates to fuel their brain with the nutrients and energy it needs to regulate their emotions. Additionally, it is recommended for children between the ages of 6 and 12 to sleep 9 to 12 hours per 24 hours. When a child's physiological needs are met, it has a positive effect on their mood and ability to regulate their emotions.

Sometimes, we might notice that we are hungry, angry, lonely, or tired, but don't have the ability to solve the problem in that moment. When that is the case, it is helpful to keep in mind that our feelings and urges are likely to be extra strong. We can use relaxation exercises such as Belly Button Breathing to help us stay calm and in control until we have the ability to take care of our HALT needs.

Being aware of our urges and the things that can make them stronger helps us to stay in control of them!

CHAPTER 9
TAKING CONTROL OF MY ACTIONS

Before I learned how to be in control of my actions, I often reacted to stressful situations in ways that made problems worse and sometimes even created new problems.

One day, the kid sitting behind me in class was repeatedly tapping his pencil on the desk. I felt so annoyed and turned around and yelled at him. It makes sense that I had the urge to yell when I was feeling annoyed, but making that choice was not good for me. I ended up getting in trouble, which made me feel even worse.

When this happened again another day, I still felt annoyed and had the urge to yell at him, but I stopped, took some deep breaths to calm down, and made the choice to turn around and politely ask him to please stop tapping on the desk. That caused him to apologize and stop tapping. The problem was solved, and I felt much better.

Whenever I am faced with a trigger, I can 1. STOP: Do something to calm down and identify the trigger, my thoughts, and my feelings, 2. THINK: Identify the different choices I can make to deal with it, and 3. GO: Identify what each choice is likely to cause, and choose my action!

Stop, Think, and Go Charts are tools that help me to choose my actions when dealing with triggers in the moment. I also like to fill out Stop, Think, and Go Charts after I've reacted to a trigger in a way that I regret. This helps me to learn and grow from my mistake. Filling out Stop, Think, and Go Charts helps to train my brain to think through these steps and stay in control when dealing with triggers later. I'll tell you about a time I used a Stop, Think, and Go Chart.

I broke a vase and thought, "I'm so clumsy! I'm going to get in so much trouble." I felt embarrassed, guilty, and nervous. I had the urge to blame it on my sister. I decided to do a Stop, Think, and Go Chart to help me choose my actions instead of just acting on my urge. Here is the chart I filled out:

STOP	THINK	GO
What is happening? What am I thinking? How am I feeling about it?	What are three different choices that I can make in this situation?	What will each choice cause? How will that make me feel? Circle the choice that would be best for me.
I broke a vase. **Thought:** "I'm so clumsy! I'm going to get in so much trouble!" **Feelings:** Embarrassed (8), Guilty (8), Nervous (8)	**1.** I can blame it on my sister. **2.** I can hide it and hope my parents don't notice. **3.** I can tell my parents and apologize for accidentally breaking it.	**1.** She could get in trouble for something that she didn't do. I would feel even guiltier. She would be mad at me. I could get caught and get into even bigger trouble. **2.** I could get away with it. I would still feel guilty and nervous about them finding it. I would probably eventually get caught and get into even bigger trouble. **3.** They would probably forgive me.

Filling out the Stop, Think, and Go Chart helped me to choose to tell my parents and apologize for accidentally breaking the vase. Although they were a little upset and scolded me for playing with my ball in the living room, they forgave me. My parents felt proud of me for telling them what happened and I felt proud of myself.

ACTIVITY
STOP, THINK, AND GO CHARTS

Read the stories and complete Stop, Think, and Go Charts for them.

1. It's raining. I come home and realize that I left my bedroom window open. Now there is water all over my desk and books.

STOP	THINK	GO
What is happening? What am I thinking? How am I feeling about it?	What are three different choices that I can make in this situation?	What will each choice cause? How will that make me feel? Circle the choice that would be best for me.

2. It is my sister's turn to do the dishes. She went out before doing them. My mom tells me to just do them.

STOP	THINK	GO
What is happening? What am I thinking? How am I feeling about it?	What are three different choices that I can make in this situation?	What will each choice cause? How will that make me feel? Circle the choice that would be best for me.

3. I really want a super-popular new pair of sneakers. My parents say no.

STOP	THINK	GO
What is happening? What am I thinking? How am I feeling about it?	What are three different choices that I can make in this situation?	What will each choice cause? How will that make me feel? Circle the choice that would be best for me.

NOW TRY THIS: Complete three Stop, Think, and Go Charts for your real-life situations. You can complete the chart when you're in the moment, choosing how you want to deal with a trigger. You can also complete the chart after you made a choice that was not good for you, which can help you to learn and grow from the experience.

STOP	THINK	GO
What is happening? What am I thinking? How am I feeling about it?	What are three different choices that I can make in this situation?	What will each choice cause? How will that make me feel? Circle the choice that would be best for me.

STOP	THINK	GO
What is happening? What am I thinking? How am I feeling about it?	What are three different choices that I can make in this situation?	What will each choice cause? How will that make me feel? Circle the choice that would be best for me.

STOP	THINK	GO
What is happening? What am I thinking? How am I feeling about it?	What are three different choices that I can make in this situation?	What will each choice cause? How will that make me feel? Circle the choice that would be best for me.

◇◇◇◇

Sometimes it's hard to think about the different choices that I can make when I'm faced with a trigger. My feelings become so strong, and it's hard to think about any choices other than the urge that I have. Whenever I am faced with a problem, I always have four choices. I can:

1. Try to solve the problem

2. Make myself feel better about it

3. Let it go and move on

4. Do something to make the problem worse

Thinking about these different choices helps me to realize things I can do other than acting on my urge when I'm faced with a trigger.

When I have homework to do but my sister doesn't, I feel a Feelings Thermometer 1 of annoyed. I can tolerate feeling a 1 of annoyed, so I choose to let it go and try to finish my homework as quickly as possible (but not rush, because that would make a new problem).

When the kid sitting behind me in class is kicking my chair, I feel a 3 of annoyed. I try to solve the problem by politely and strongly saying, "Can you please stop kicking my chair? Thank you!"

When Sammy has friends over and I have no plans, I feel a 5 of annoyed. I make myself feel better about the problem by telling myself that I will have friends over another day. I also do an activity that I enjoy doing alone and try to focus on that instead of thinking about the fact that I don't have friends over. That also makes me feel better.

When I try to solve a problem, the key word is *try*. It is important to remember that trying to solve a problem doesn't always fix the problem. Sometimes solving a problem takes Plan A, Plan B, Plan C—and even Plan Z. When my efforts to solve a problem don't work, I can choose to keep trying to solve the problem. I can also decide to make myself feel better about the problem or to let it go and move on. It's my choice, and I can change my decision at any point!

One night, I realized that I forgot to do a project that was due the next day. I felt overwhelmed and had the urge to avoid thinking about it. I knew that if I didn't think about the project, it wouldn't go away. This would just make things worse later. I decided to try to solve the problem. Plan A: I brought my backpack to my bedroom and started working on it. It was getting closer to bedtime, and I realized that I wasn't likely to finish it on my own. I decided to keep trying to solve the problem. Plan B: I told my parents about my problem and asked for help. My parents helped me try to get it done, but we realized that it was too much to do in one night. We came up with Plan C: I told the teacher about my mistake and asked for extra time to finish the project. The teacher said I could have extra time to finish the project, but that I was going to lose points for handing it in late. I felt disappointed. While I would have preferred the teacher to give me the extra time without taking the points away, I decided to accept that and move on. I finished the project, handed it in, and everything worked out. My grade would have been better had I turned the project in on time, but I did fine. I solved the problem as best as possible and then moved on!

When I choose to make myself feel better about the problem, I can use a tool to relax my body, I can use a tool to challenge unhelpful Feelings Monster Thoughts, or I can find another way to make my feelings less bad, such as talking to someone.

I once made a card for my friend's birthday. I worked really hard on it and felt really proud when I gave it to her. When I walked by the garbage can a few minutes later, I saw the card. I felt hurt. I had the urge to say things that would make her feel hurt too, but I knew that would just make more problems. I chose to make myself feel better about the problem. I thought of one of the helpful self-statements: "I can't control what other people do, but I can control the way that I think about it and the way that I react to it." I told myself that it was kind to make her a card, and the card I made was really good. The fact that she threw out the card didn't change that. I felt a little less bad and moved on with my day.

Sometimes when I'm faced with a trigger, I choose to let it go and move on. This is different from bottling up my feelings about it. When I move on, the feelings are no longer in my Feelings Cup.

Our teacher once told us that we were going to do an experiment in science class the following day. I love experiments and was so excited. When it came time for science class the next day, the teacher passed out a worksheet and told the class to independently complete it. I felt disappointed and annoyed. I had the urge to refuse to do the worksheet. I made the choice to let it go and move on. I finished the worksheet and moved on with my day.

While most people would not choose to make a problem worse on purpose, this is what usually happens when we make the choice to act on our urges.

One day, I was in the middle of playing a game, and my mom suddenly told me that we had to leave for a dentist appointment. I wasn't given any warning. I didn't even know I had a dentist appointment that day. I felt frustrated and annoyed. I had the urge to respond, "No! That's so unfair! I'm not going!" I acted on my urge. This caused my mom and me to argue, for us to be late to the appointment, and for me to get in trouble. When we got home, I wasn't allowed to play my game anymore. Choosing to act on my urge caused me to have even more problems to deal with: an argument with my mom, being late, and being in trouble.

NOTE TO THE GROWN-UPS: Transitions are a common trigger. While it can be especially difficult for children to switch from a preferred activity to doing something that they need to do, even transitions between activities that a child enjoys can be overwhelming sometimes. Children benefit from being able to anticipate when a transition is coming.

Try to follow routines when possible. Provide your child with transitional warnings so that they have time to mentally prepare to shift gears. For example, you can give your child a 20-minute warning before dinnertime, followed by a 5-minute warning, a 1-minute warning, and then a 5-second countdown. Of course, life happens, and it is not always possible to give transitional warnings.

In the example provided, perhaps Alex's mother forgot about the dentist appointment until last minute. In such cases, validating your child's feelings can be powerful. Alex's mother could have said, "I know it's a bummer to have to stop playing and leave with no warning. That's so frustrating." Feeling heard and understood can help children to tolerate stressful situations. Transitions that go smoothly are great opportunities to praise the positive choices that your child made.

It doesn't feel like it's a choice when we act on our urges, but remember, everything we do is a choice. It can be hard to choose not to act on an urge. If we practice the tools and skills to take control of our thinking, feelings, and behavior, we can get better at choosing our actions when faced with a trigger!

ACTIVITY
THE FOUR CHOICES WHEN FACED WITH A PROBLEM

Read the stories. Come up with a specific way that you could make each choice to respond. Circle the choice that you would make in each situation.

1. I'm playing with my friends. It's time for me to go home, but my friends are all still playing and I want to stay.

Try to solve the problem:

_____

_____

_____

_____

Make myself feel better about the problem:

_____

_____

_____

_____

Let it go and move on:

_____

_____

_____

_____

Do something to make the problem worse:

_____

_____

_____

_____

2. I thought I did well on a test. I received a much lower grade than I expected.

Try to solve the problem:

_____

_____

_____

_____

Make myself feel better about the problem:

_____

_____

_____

_____

Let it go and move on:

_____

_____

_____

_____

Do something to make the problem worse:

_____

_____

_____

_____

THE SELF-REGULATION WORKBOOK FOR KIDS

3. My friend accuses me of lying. I did not lie.

Try to solve the problem:

_____

_____

_____

_____

Make myself feel better about the problem:

_____

_____

_____

_____

Let it go and move on:

_____

_____

_____

_____

Do something to make the problem worse:

_____

_____

_____

_____

NOW TRY THIS: Come up with ways you can make each choice to deal with three of your real-life situations. You can do this to help you brainstorm ways to deal with a situation that you are in the process of dealing with. You can also do this to reflect on situations that you've handled in the past or that you think you might deal with in the future.

1. _____

Try to solve the problem:

_____

_____

_____

_____

Make myself feel better about the problem:

_____

_____

_____

_____

Let it go and move on:

_____

_____

_____

_____

Do something to make the problem worse:

_____

_____

_____

_____

2. _____

Try to solve the problem:

_____

_____

_____

_____

Make myself feel better about the problem:

_____

_____

_____

_____

Let it go and move on:

_____

_____

_____

Do something to make the problem worse:

_____

_____

_____

3. _____

Try to solve the problem:

_____

_____

_____

_____

Make myself feel better about the problem:

_____

_____

_____

_____

Let it go and move on:

_____

_____

_____

_____

Do something to make the problem worse:

_____

_____

_____

_____

◇◇◇◇

I can choose my actions by thinking about what I want to cause. Sometimes when my feelings are really strong, it is hard to think about the big picture. My brain gets focused on what I want to cause in the moment. Identifying and thinking about what I want to cause can help me to make choices that are better for me.

These are some of the things I like to consider when thinking about what I want to cause:

- How do I want people to describe me?

  o Kind

  o Cool

  o Talented

- What do I want to cause at home?

  o To have fun

  o For my family to feel proud of me

  o What do I want to cause at school?

  o To get good grades

  o To learn new things

  o To have good friends

- What do I want to cause in my life?

  o To help people and animals

  o To become a veterinarian

ACTIVITY
CHOOSING MY ACTIONS BY THINKING ABOUT WHAT I WANT TO CAUSE

Write two choices that Alex can make to take himself closer to each of the things that he wants to cause.

WHAT ALEX WANTS TO CAUSE	CHOICES ALEX CAN MAKE
To be kind	1. 2.
To be cool	1. 2.
To be talented	1. 2.
To have fun	1. 2.
For his family to feel proud of him	1. 2.
To get good grades	1. 2.
To learn new things	1. 2.
To have good friends	1. 2.

To help people and animals	1.
	2.
To become a veterinarian	1.
	2.

NOW TRY THIS: Identify the things you want to cause in the different areas of your life.

How do I want people to describe me?

_____

_____

_____

_____

What do I want to cause at home?

_____

_____

_____

_____

What do I want to cause at school?

_____

_____

_____

_____

　THE SELF-REGULATION WORKBOOK FOR KIDS

What do I want to cause in my life?

_____

_____

_____

_____

NOW TRY THIS: Write each thing you want to cause on the chart. Identify two choices that you can make for each one. Once you have identified the choices you can make to take yourself closer to the things you want to cause, you can put them on a to-do list and make an effort to do them!

WHAT I WANT TO CAUSE	CHOICES I CAN MAKE
	1. 2.
	1. 2.
	1. 2.
	1. 2.
	1. 2.
	1. 2.
	1. 2.

	1.
	2.
	1.
	2.
	1.
	2.

While every choice I make doesn't directly connect with each of these things I want to cause, I can think about whether my choices will take me closer to or further away from causing them.

◇◇◇◇

In the morning, I'm usually really tired and comfortable and don't want to get out of bed. If I filled out a Stop, Think, and Go Chart in that moment, it would probably look like this:

STOP	THINK	GO
What is happening? What am I thinking? How am I feeling about it?	What are three different choices that I can make in this situation?	What will each choice cause? How will that make me feel? Circle the choice that would be best for me.
It's time to get out of bed and get ready for school. Thought: "I want to sleep more." Feelings: Tired, comfortable, and annoyed	**1.** Go back to sleep. **2.** Get up and complain about having to wake up all morning until I get to school. **3.** Get up, put on my favorite music, and do some jumping jacks before getting ready to go to school.	**1.** I'd feel comfortable and less tired. **2.** I'd feel tired and annoyed. My family would feel annoyed and tell me to stop complaining. I'd get to school. **3.** I'd feel tired and annoyed, followed by a little burst of energy. I'd get to school.

While feeling comfortable and less tired seems like the best thing to cause in that moment, choosing to go back to sleep would take me further away from the things I want to cause in the big picture. If I go back to bed instead of going to school, I could miss out on fun opportunities in school, so this choice would take me further away from having fun. It would also take me further away from my family feeling proud of me, getting good grades, and learning cool things. I need to work hard in school to become a veterinarian, so going back to bed would even take me further away from that life goal! When I consider all of these things, my Stop, Think, and Go Chart would look like this:

STOP	THINK	GO
What is happening? What am I thinking? How am I feeling about it?	What are three different choices that I can make in this situation?	What will each choice cause? How will that make me feel? Circle the choice that would be best for me.
It's time to get out of bed and get ready for school. Thought: "I want to sleep more." **Feelings:** Tired, comfortable, and annoyed	**1.** Go back to sleep. **2.** Get up and complain about having to wake up all morning until I get to school. **3.** Get up, put on my favorite music, and do some jumping jacks before getting ready to go to school.	**1.** I'd feel comfortable and less tired. **2.** I'd feel tired and annoyed. My family would feel annoyed and tell me to stop complaining. I'd get to school. **3.** I'd feel tired and annoyed, followed by a little burst of energy. I'd get to school.

To help me think through this, I like to use the Choice Rating Scale. Choices rated 1 are choices that take me closer to the things I want to cause. Choices rated 2 are choices that do not take me closer to or further away from the things I want to cause. Choices rated 3 are choices that take me further away from the things I want to cause.

THE CHOICE RATING SCALE
1. This choice will take me closer to the things I want to cause.
2. This choice will not take me closer to or further away from the things I want to cause.
3. This choice will take me further away from the things I want to cause.

In that situation, going back to sleep is rated 3. It takes me further away from the things I want to cause. Getting up and complaining about having to wake up all morning until I get to school is also rated 3. Although it would take me closer to getting good grades and learning cool things, it takes me further away from having fun. It's certainly not fun for my family when I complain, and is likely to result in people feeling annoyed and reacting in ways that aren't fun for me. Some choices take us closer to some of the things we want to cause but further away from others. Sometimes these are the best choices to make, especially when we can't think of a choice for a situation that would be rated a 1. That wasn't the case in this situation, however. Getting up, putting on my favorite music, and doing some jumping jacks before getting ready to go to school is rated 1. It takes me closer to having fun, my family feeling proud of me, getting good grades, and learning cool things. It does not take me further away from any of the things I want to cause.

ACTIVITY
RATE THE CHOICES

Think about the things that Alex wants to cause. Rate the choices for Alex.

THE THINGS ALEX WANTS TO CAUSE	THE CHOICE RATING SCALE
• To be kind • To be cool • To be talented • To have fun • For my family to feel proud of me • To get good grades • To learn new things • To have good friends • To help people and animals • To become a veterinarian	**1.** This choice will take me closer to the things I want to cause **2.** This choice will not take me closer to or further away from the things I want to cause **3.** This choice will take me further away from the things I want to cause

THE SITUATION	CHOICE	RATING
1. My friend teases a classmate.	I laugh.	
2. It's the weekend, and I don't have anything planned.	I sleep in.	
3. My parents tell me to take a bath, but I don't want to.	I take a bath as quickly as possible.	
4. I notice a kid sitting alone at lunch.	I ask him if he wants to sit at my lunch table.	
5. Class is boring.	I zone out and doodle.	

Answers:

1. 3, 2. 2, 3. 1, 4. 1, 5. 3

NOW TRY THIS: Rate five choices that you made this week. Use the list you previously wrote of things you want to cause to guide your ratings.

THE SITUATION	CHOICE	RATING
1.		
2.		
3.		
4.		
5.		

◇◇◇◇

Sometimes I like to write things I want to cause in specific situations or for specific upcoming plans that I have.

When we went to visit family, I wanted to cause these things:

- To have fun

- To play with my cousins

- For my cousins to think I'm cool

While we were there, I was playing basketball with my two older cousins. They kept passing the ball back and forth to each other. Fifteen minutes passed and I still never had a turn with the ball. I felt frustrated and hurt that they were leaving me out. I had the urge to yell at them. Yelling at my cousins would be rated 3 because it would take me further away from having fun, further away from playing with my cousins, and further away from my cousins thinking I'm cool. Luckily, I had a plan for how I could deal with this trigger!

When I know a specific trigger that I might be faced with, I like to come up with a plan for how I can deal with it. It also helps me to practice this plan before facing the trigger.

There have been times in the past when I was hanging with my older cousins and I felt left out. When this happened, it triggered strong feelings for me, and I acted on urges that made the situation worse. Since I know feeling left out with my older cousins is a trigger that is sometimes hard for me to deal with, I came up with a plan for how I could deal with it.

- First, I identified the trigger: feeling left out.

- Next, I identified the emotions this brings up for me and how strong they get on the Feelings Thermometer. When this happened in the past, I felt an 8 of frustrated and a 6 of hurt.

- I identified how this felt in my body: my fists clenched up, my shoulders got tight and tense, and my breath got short and shallow in my chest. I chose a relaxation exercise to help me chill out these feelings in my body.

- Next, I identified the Automatic Thoughts I had. I thought, "They're such jerks! They always leave me out! They deserve to be punished!" I came up with a Challenge Thought: "I wish they included me, but they're not jerks, and it's probably not personal. They're both older than me and really into basketball. They might not even realize they're leaving me out. Trying to punish them would only make things worse."

- I identified the urges this trigger gives me: to yell at them, call them jerks, and storm off. Knowing what urges I might have helps me to be more aware and in control if I have them.

- Next, I came up with a better choice that I can make to deal with the situation. I decided that I would like to try to solve the problem by saying, "Hey, guys! Can I have a chance with the ball too?" in a strong, but chill manner.

- Since trying to solve a problem doesn't always work, I also came up with a Plan B: to let it go, move on, and go find something else that's fun to do until they're done playing basketball.

After coming up with this plan, I practiced by acting it out. Practicing a plan by actually rehearsing each step helps me to use it more effectively when I am faced with the trigger.

Sure enough, I was faced with this trigger when we visited my family. I had strong feelings, Feelings Monster Thoughts, and urges that would have made the problem worse, but I had the power to stay calm and in control at the same time! I followed the plan just like I practiced it! My cousins apologized, passed me the ball, and I ended up having so much fun playing with them!

NOTE TO THE GROWN-UPS: It is helpful for you to role play the Trigger Response Plans with your child. When plans involve the child expressing themselves, be sure to help them understand and practice using the appropriate body language and tone of voice for the situation.

ACTIVITY
TRIGGER RESPONSE PLANS

Identify three triggers that are difficult for you to deal with. Write a Trigger Response Plan for each one. Rehearse following the plan with a grown-up.

1. Trigger: _____

    Feelings caused and rating on the Feelings Thermometer:

_____

_____

_____

_____

    Feelings in my body:

_____

_____

_____

_____

    Relaxation exercises or coping skills to help chill out the feelings:

_____

_____

_____

_____

Automatic Thoughts:

_____

_____

_____

_____

Challenge Thoughts (write these on a notecard if that would be helpful):

_____

_____

_____

_____

Urges:

_____

_____

_____

_____

Planned Response:

_____

_____

_____

_____

Plan B:

_____

_____

_____

_____

2. Trigger: _____

Feelings caused and rating on the Feelings Thermometer:

_____

_____

_____

_____

Feelings in my body:

_____

_____

_____

_____

Relaxation exercises or coping skills to help chill out the feelings:

_____

_____

_____

_____

Automatic Thoughts:

_____

_____

_____

_____

Challenge Thoughts (write these on a notecard if that would be helpful):

_____

_____

_____

_____

Urges:

_____

_____

_____

_____

Planned Response:

_____

_____

_____

_____

THE SELF-REGULATION WORKBOOK FOR KIDS

Plan B:

_____

_____

_____

_____

3. Trigger: _____

Feelings caused and rating on the Feelings Thermometer:

_____

_____

_____

_____

Feelings in my body:

_____

_____

_____

_____

Relaxation exercises or coping skills to help chill out the feelings:

_____

_____

_____

_____

Automatic Thoughts:

_____

_____

_____

_____

Challenge Thoughts (write these on a notecard if that would be helpful):

_____

_____

_____

_____

Urges:

_____

_____

_____

_____

Planned Response:

_____

_____

_____

_____

Plan B:

_____

_____

_____

_____

NOTE TO THE GROWN-UPS: Whenever possible, tell other adults in your child's support network about your child's triggers and plans for coping with them. This can include babysitters, grandparents, teachers, school counselors, coaches, and the parents of your child's close friends.

◇◇◇◇

CHAPTER 10
MY STORY: WHEN MY FEELINGS WERE IN CONTROL

Fill in the blanks to write a story about a time when your feelings took control.

Hi! I'm _____. Every day, I experience lots of feelings.
               (your name)

Some feelings I experience are _____,
                                    (a feeling)

_____, _____,
   (a different feeling)   (a different feeling)

_____, and _____. It's normal and
   (a different feeling)   (a different feeling)

okay to experience all different feelings! My feelings can affect the feelings in my

body, the things I think, and the actions I want to take. I can have a feeling and

be in control at the same time, but sometimes it's hard to stay in control. This is

a story about a time I felt _____, and the feelings were in
                              (a feeling)

control.

One day, _____. I thought,
                 trigger–something that happened

"_____." I felt
              automatic thought

_____. The feeling was this strong on the Feelings
   (a feeling)

Thermometer:

Mark how strong the feeling was.

10	Exploding
9	
8	Really strong feelings
7	
6	I'm feeling it
5	
4	
3	Beginning to feel it
2	
1	Not feeling it

My body felt like this:
Illustrate the feelings in your body.

I _____.
urge/action that you did

After I acted on that urge, it caused _____
What happened? How did others feel? How did others react?

_____

_____.

This made me feel _____.
feeling

Sometimes feelings take control and I act on my urges, which usually makes the problem worse. When this happens, I can do something to repair and move on. I can also learn from this experience, which can help me to be more in control of my feelings in the future!

After my feelings took control in this situation, I repaired by _____

_____.

something you can say and/or do to repair

Something that I learned from this experience was_____

_____.

This experience was stressful, but I can move on and try to stay more in control of

my feelings in the future!

CHAPTER 11
MY STORY: WHEN I TOOK CONTROL OF MY FEELINGS

Fill in the blanks to rewrite the story about when your feelings were in control. This time, you will be taking control of the feelings!

Hi! I'm _____. Every day, I experience lots of feelings.
          (your name)

Some feelings I experience are _____,
                                      (a feeling)

_____, _____,
   (a different feeling)   (a different feeling)

_____, and _____. It's normal and
   (a different feeling)   (a different feeling)

okay to experience all different feelings! My feelings can affect the feelings in my

body, the things I think, and the actions I want to take. I can have a feeling and

be in control at the same time, but sometimes it's hard to stay in control. This is

a story about a time I felt _____, and the feelings were in
                                   (a feeling)

control.

One day, _____. I thought,
              trigger—something that happened

"_____." I felt
                   automatic thought

_____. The feeling was this strong on the Feelings
        (a feeling)

Thermometer:

Mark how strong the feeling was.

10	Exploding
9	
8	Really strong feelings
7	
6	I'm feeling it
5	
4	
3	Beginning to feel it
2	
1	Not feeling it

My body felt like this:
Illustrate the feelings in your body.

I had the urge to _____.
                              urge

I knew that it would not be good for me to act on this urge, so I used some coping tools to take control.

First, I did _____ to calm down the
                        a relaxation exercise

feelings in my body.

I realized that _____ was an
                              automatic thought

unhelpful Feelings Monster Thought, so I talked back to it! I said, "_____

_____."
              challenge thought

I still felt _____, but the feeling wasn't as
                              feeling

strong as before. The feeling became this strong on the Feelings Thermometer:

10	Exploding
9	
8	Really strong feelings
7	
6	I'm feeling it
5	
4	Beginning to feel it
3	
2	
1	Not feeling it

I could have the feeling and be in control at the same time!

I thought of some other choices that I could make to deal with the trigger. I chose

to _____.
choice

After I made this choice, it caused _____
What happened? How did others feel? How did others react?

_____

_____.

This made me feel _____.
feeling

I am Super _____! I have the power to
your name

take control of my feelings!

CHAPTER 12

I HAVE THE POWER TO TAKE CONTROL OF MY FEELINGS, THINKING, AND ACTIONS!

We may not be superheroes, but having the skills to be in control of our feelings, thinking, and actions gives us real power to do great things! Draw a picture of yourself as a superhero. Keep this in mind to help you feel empowered to deal with whatever situations and feelings come your way.

I have the power to be in control of my thinking, feelings, and actions!

GLOSSARY

5, 4, 3, 2, 1: A grounding activity that supports bringing the mind to the moment. Allowing thoughts to drift to the past and the future can trigger more intense unpleasant emotions, which makes it more difficult to manage them. This tool helps to focus thoughts and emotions based on what's happening in that moment.

All-or-Nothing Thinking: A common unhelpful thinking pattern of seeing things in black-and-white categories, as either good or bad. With All-or-Nothing Thinking, it has to be one way or it is seen as not okay.

Automatic Thoughts: The thoughts or images that instantly pop in mind when something happens. People are often unaware of these thoughts, which can shape their emotions and actions, even if they are not always based on reality.

Belly Button Breathing: A relaxation exercise that helps to calm the body by slowing down the breathing and ensuring that the belly is rising and falling with each breath.

Broken Record Player Thinking: A common unhelpful pattern of thinking about something on repeat that may be true but is not helpful to focus on.

Challenge Thought: A statement used to respond to an automatic Feelings Monster Thought. Challenge Thoughts directly address the parts of the Automatic Thought that are not based on reality and that trigger a person to feel worse. It is important for Challenge Thoughts to be believable.

Choice Rating Scale: A tool that helps people to choose their actions by rating them on a scale of 1 to 3 based on what they want to cause. Those rated 1 take us closer to the things we want to cause, while those rated 3 take use further away.

Delayed Gratification: Passing the opportunity for an immediate reward to feel even more satisfied and rewarded in the future.

Disqualifying the Positive: A common unhelpful pattern of thinking positive things do not count for one reason or another.

Emotional Reasoning: A common unhelpful thinking pattern of believing something must be true just because you feel that way, even if there are no facts that support the belief.

Feelings Cube: A cube that has a different emotion on each side. The cube is rolled or thrown like a die. This can be used to play games to help people identify, understand, and explore their emotions.

Feelings Cup: An image of a cup filled with liquid that represents how much room a person has to hold feelings. The cup represents a person's capacity for holding feelings and the liquid represents the feelings. When the cup is very full, it represents a person holding on to a lot of feelings. This makes it more likely for the feelings to overflow, which represents a maladaptive emotional reaction.

Feelings Explosion: When feelings come out as a maladaptive behavior. When a person has a Feelings Explosion, they do not think about their actions before doing them.

Feel-Good File: A place to collect items with reminders of one's positive qualities and strengths. A Feel-Good File can help to challenge unhelpful thoughts that trigger people to feel bad about themselves.

Feelings Monster Thoughts: Automatic unhelpful thoughts that are not based on reality. This type of thinking shapes emotions in a maladaptive manner, often triggering more intense negative emotions about the situation someone is thinking about, which makes it more challenging for them to respond to the situation in an effective manner.

Feelings Thermometer: A tool that looks like a standard thermometer used for measuring the temperature, but is used instead to measure how strong an emotion is experienced.

Fight, Flight, or Freeze reaction: The automatic response that happens in the body when faced with a perceived threat. This is helpful when there is actually something to protect ourselves from by fighting, running away, or freezing. This is unhelpful in situations that trigger us to feel threatened but do not require us to take any of these actions to protect ourselves.

HALT: People can use this acronym for Hungry, Angry, Lonely, and Tired to remember to check if they are feeling any of these things. When any of these experiences are not being addressed, it negatively impacts the ability to cope with our feelings in a healthy manner. Addressing hunger, anger, loneliness, and fatigue can place us in a better state to navigate distressing situations in a healthy manner.

Helpful Self-statements: Prepared statements that support our ability to view stressful situations in a more adaptive manner that is based on reality as opposed to being based on emotions. These thoughts are often created to directly challenge Repeat Offender Thoughts or common unhelpful thoughts.

Instant Gratification: Something that makes a person feel satisfied or rewarded in the moment.

Instant Mood Shifter: Something a person can think about that makes them feel happy, calm, or relaxed. An Instant Mood Shifter helps people to shift their thinking away from thoughts that make them feel bad, which helps to shift their mood. We can fill files or folders with objects that bring us joy to use as Instant Mood Shifters.

Joy Journal: A daily record of the experiences that have brought a person joy. Keeping this record can shift their thinking in a way that helps them to acknowledge and thus experience more joy.

Labeling: A common unhelpful pattern of seeing oneself as something negative when describing a mistake. Another form of labeling occurs when attaching a negative label to a person who does something one does not like. When people label and mislabel, they describe things with words that are loaded with feelings.

Magnification or Minimization: A common unhelpful pattern of blowing up the importance of or shrinking things until they seem tiny.

Mental Filter: A common unhelpful pattern of picking out and focusing only on a negative detail. Like a drop of ink that changes the color of an entire cup of water, this type of thinking darkens the way people see things.

Mental vacation: A tool that involves imagining a place that makes you feel calm and relaxed in as many details as possible. This tool can support a shift in mood by shifting the thinking.

Mind Reading: A common unhelpful thinking pattern of assuming that someone is having negative thoughts about you.

One-Nostril Breathing: A relaxation exercise that helps to calm down the body by breathing slowly through one nostril.

Overgeneralization: A common unhelpful thinking pattern of seeing a single negative event as a never-ending pattern of defeat. One thinks this is always going to happen, or this will always be the way it is.

Personalization: A common unhelpful thinking pattern of blaming oneself for something negative that happened or someone else's negative behavior, even if it's possible or likely that there's another explanation.

Repeat Offender Thoughts: An unhelpful thought that comes up again and again. Identifying these thoughts improves the ability to notice when they arise and be prepared to challenge them.

Shake and Roll Out the Stress: A relaxation exercise that helps to calm down the body by shaking and rolling the hands, head, and shoulders.

"Should" and "Must" Statements: A common unhelpful thinking pattern of thinking there is a certain way that everyone should do things and making it a big deal when things don't go the way you think they should.

Stop, Think, and Go Charts: A tool that helps people to choose their actions when faced with a trigger.

Toy Breathing: A relaxation exercise that helps to calm down the bodies by using a toy to help make sure that the belly is rising and falling with each breath.

Trigger: A situation, person, place, or thing that causes a reaction. Our reactions can include emotions, thoughts, feelings in our bodies, and behaviors.

The Chair Technique: A relaxation exercise that helps to calm down the body by purposefully tensing the muscles while sitting in a chair and then releasing the tension.

The Fortune-Teller Error: A common unhelpful thinking pattern of thinking that things will turn out badly and have feelings as if the bad thing is definitely going to happen. One believes they can't deal with the bad thing if it happens, even if it would just be uncomfortable.

The Ragdoll Technique: A relaxation exercise also known as Progressive Muscle Relaxation that helps to calm down the body by purposefully tensing each muscle and then releasing the tension.

Thought Challenge Worksheet: A worksheet that includes a number of questions to help assess and challenge unhelpful thoughts.

Thought Records: A tool that helps to challenge unhelpful thoughts and increase awareness about how those thoughts are shaping the emotions.

Trigger Response Plans: A specific plan for dealing with a trigger. This plan is written down and rehearsed, which helps one to be more prepared to cope with the trigger when faced with it in real life.

Tunnel vision: A common unhelpful thinking pattern of seeing the parts of a situation that are bad.

Urge: A desire to do something. You can have an urge and choose not to act on it.

REFERENCES

Beck, Judith S. *Cognitive Behavior Therapy, Second Edition: Basics and Beyond*. New York; The Guilford Press, 2021.

Greene, Ross W. *Explosive Child: A New Approach for Understanding and Parenting Easily Frustrated, Chronically Inflexible Children*. New York: HarperCollins, 2021.

Linehan, Marsha M. *DBT® Skills Training Handouts and Worksheets*, Second Edition. New York, NY: The Guilford Press, 2015.

Linehan, Marsha M. *DBT Skills Training Manual*, Second Edition. New York, NY: The Guilford Press, 2015.

Mazza, James J., Elizabeth T. Dexter-Mazza, Alec L. Miller, Jill H. Rathus, Heather E. Murphy, and Marsha M. Linehan. *DBT Skills in Schools: Skills Training for Emotional Problem Solving for Adolescents (DBT STEPS-A)*. New York: The Guilford Press, 2016.

Miller, Alec L. and Jill H. Rathus. *DBT Skills Manual for Adolescents*. New York: The Guilford Press, 2017.

Sokol, Leslie, and Marci G. Fox. *The Comprehensive Clinician's Guide to Cognitive Behavioral Therapy*. Eau Claire, WI: PESI Publishing & Media, 2020.

Zucker, Bonnie. *Anxiety-Free Kids: An Interactive Guide for Parents and Children*. Waco, TX: Prufrock Press, Inc., 2017.

ACKNOWLEDGMENTS

This book has been shaped by the people I have worked with throughout my career. The children, family members, teachers, and others who gave me the opportunity to understand their unique experiences have taught me so much. Thank you to all of my former clients, supervisors, supervisees, and colleagues for the innumerable conversations that have helped me to become a better clinician and a better person.

Thank you to Amber Hickey and Anneliese Abel, my friends and consultants, who provided feedback that helped to ensure that the work was accessible to parents and children. Keren Ludwig, my clinical supervisor, mentor, and friend, always provided me with the encouragement and confidence to take professional leaps. Tovah Miller and Rachel Gitlin offered a constant chain of feedback and championing as I wrote this book.

I appreciate Renee Rutledge and Claire Sielaff at Ulysses Press for this opportunity and offering guidance along the way. Joan Garry, Cindy Pereira, and Jen Garry generously offered advice as I entered the world of writing.

My parents, Michael and Elyse Berman, have provided a lifetime of indispensable support that has paved the path for all of the work that I have done.

I could not have written this book without the endless support from my partner Colin Garry throughout the process. My daughter Natasha was a constant source of inspiration.

ABOUT THE AUTHOR

Jenna Berman is a therapist based in New York City and New Jersey. She received a bachelor's degree in psychology from Hobart and William Smith Colleges, a master's degree in social work from Columbia University, and post-graduate training at the Ackerman Institute for the Family and NYU. Jenna has a range of experience working in outpatient mental health, school, residential, and medical settings. She is passionate about helping children and adolescents feel empowered to overcome obstacles and reach their potential. She currently resides in Montclair, New Jersey, with her partner Colin, their daughter Natasha, and their two cats Benson and Stabler.